P9-DBK-236

The Lorette Wilmot Library
Nazareth College of Rochester

Persius

Twayne's World Authors Series
Latin Literature

Philip Levine, Editor
University of California, Los Angeles

TWAS 713

Folio 1a from the 1494 Venice edition of Persius with the commentary of Bartolomeo Fonte. Persius, garlanded with the poet's laurel wreath, is seated at a medieval teacher's desk in the center dictating to his two early Italian commentators. Fonte (seen on the right in deep thought) and Johannes Britannicus of Brescia, who is writing on the left. *By permission of the Houghton Library, Harvard University.*

Persius

By Mark Morford

The Ohio State University

Twayne Publishers · Boston

Persius

Mark Morford

Copyright © 1984 by G. K. Hall & Company
All Rights Reserved
Published by Twayne Publishers
A Division of G. K. Hall & Company
70 Lincoln Street
Boston, Massachusetts 02111

Printed on permanent/durable acid-
free paper and bound in the United
States of America.

Library of Congress Cataloging in Publication Data

Morford, Mark P. O., 1929–
  Persius.

  Bibliography: p.
  Includes index.
  1. Persius—Criticism and interpretation.   I. Title.
PA6556.M67   1984   871'.01   84-537
ISBN 0-8057-6560-3

Contents

About the Author

Mark Morford was educated in England, where he earned the B.A. and M.A. degrees at the University of Oxford, and the Ph.D. degree in classics at the University of London. He taught in private schools in England and the United States from 1952 until 1963, when he joined the Department of Classics at the Ohio State University. He was promoted to the rank of professor in 1969, and served as chairman of the department from 1968 until 1980. He has served on many professional boards and has been consultant to a number of departments of classics. He was president of the Classical Association of the Middle West and South in 1981-82. He has published two Latin readers and is the joint author, with Robert J. Lenardon, of Classical Mythology (second edition, 1977). He directed a four-year developmental program in Greek and Roman Civilizations, 1976-80, funded by the National Endowment for the Humanities, and is a coauthor of materials in that program, published by the Charles Merrill Co. in 1980. He was appointed professor of classics at the University of Virginia in 1984.

His major area of research is Latin literature, and his book, The Poet Lucan, was published in 1967. He has published a number of articles on satire, on the Neronian Age and its problems, and on a number of other aspects of Roman literature and history. He has also written several articles on Greek tragedy and the Greek orators.

Preface

Persius is undervalued as a poet by historians of Roman satire. Even more than his contemporary, the epic poet Lucan, he has suffered from ridicule and neglect since the seventeenth century. The standard German handbook for Latin literature ends the article on Persius with the words, "It is with relief that one lays Persius aside," and even those who are more sympathetic tend to excuse him for his youth rather than to examine objectively the style and content of his satires. Persius died when he was twenty-seven, yet critics generally overlook the fact that Horace was only thirty when his first book of satires was published, as was Boileau when his first seven satires were published in 1666; Pope's _Essay on Criticism_ and _Rape of the Lock_ were published before the poet was twenty-five. This book seeks to show that Persius's youth has little to do with the shortcomings of his style, while his poetry is the product of a master who deliberately wrote as he did.

The decline in Persius's fortunes began with the powerful criticism of J. C. Scaliger in his _Poetics_, published in 1567, and in the English-speaking world it was made seemingly irreversible by the authoritative essay of John Dryden (_A Discourse concerning the Original and Progress of Satire_), which was published in 1693. In between these two works appeared the great edition of Persius by Isaac Casaubon (1605) whose preface remains to this day one of the most discerning analyses of the nature of satire. It was Casaubon's defense of Persius that Dryden attacked in his _Discourse_. Dryden himself preferred Juvenal of the three surviving Latin hexameter-satirists, and in the great age of English satire it was Horace and Juvenal whom Pope, Johnson, and their contemporaries imitated. Since then Persius has been studied less and less, and in the present century the decline of Latin studies in general has made it even less likely that as difficult a writer as Persius should be popular.

All this has developed in the last few centuries. For well over a thousand years Persius was read and admired. His book of poems, in all amounting to less than seven hundred lines, immediately became the equivalent of a "best-seller" and was one of the classical works that were regularly read in schools. Even with the triumph of Christianity Persius continued to be read and quoted, and manuscript copies of his works were constantly being made. At the threshold of the Italian Renaissance Dante placed Persius in the very small group of classical poets (including Homer) who, although non-Christian, were worthy teachers of morality. Paradoxically it was with the spread of knowledge of the Greek and Roman classics that Persius began to lose ground, and, as we have seen, by the eighteenth century he had become relegated to the ranks of the minor classical poets.

The study of Persius involves three main areas: satiric quality, style (which includes poetic techniques and language), and ethical quality. In antiquity, including the early Christian centuries, his style was recognized as difficult, but in a world where men still thought and spoke in Latin this was not considered an insuperable handicap. At all times his ethical qualities have been admired, and after the triumph of Christianity it was this aspect of his achievement that dominated attitudes toward him. There were few exceptions, and of the Christian Fathers perhaps only Jerome, himself no mean satirist, really appreciated the satirist in Persius, as opposed to the moral preceptor. Since the time of Scaliger Persius's style has been the main area of concern. His obscurity, real or imagined, has been the pretext for dismissing him from the trinity of extant Latin hexameter-satirists, leaving the field to Horace and Juvenal. The urbane friendliness of Horace was foreign to Persius, perhaps temperamentally and certainly in the light of his very different social circumstances. Persius's elitist view of the poet's audience was bound to increase his isolation from a wider public, as he himself foresaw. At the same time his style lacked the rhetorical force and moral indignation that made Juvenal the most powerful of satirists. Therefore Persius has been, as it were, squeezed out between his urbane predecessor and his forceful successor.

This book has grown from twenty years' study of the

Age of Nero. It was by any standards an age of remarkable cultural achievement. It has long been fashionable, however, to judge Neronian literature unfavorably by the criterion of Augustan literature. According to this approach Lucan, the greatest literary genius of Nero's time, is to be condemned in comparison with Vergil, Persius in comparison with Horace. Seneca, because of his ambiguous public career, is not widely admired, and only Petronius is today generally read with approval. This valuation would hardly have been understood in Renaissance Europe (especially England and France in the sixteenth and seventeenth centuries), much less in earlier centuries. Dante, for example, made Cato of Utica (the great Stoic hero, especially admired by the Stoics of Nero's time) no less than a guardian in the Christian Purgatory, specifically because of the Stoic emphasis upon liberty and individual dignity that was so prominent a feature of the best Neronian literature. It is important, therefore, to have a fair idea of the times in which Persius lived. Accordingly, the first chapter of the present study sets his life in the context of the events and debates of the reign of Nero. It discusses the members of Persius's circle, some of whom were influential men, and gives a succinct view of the principal features of the reign of Nero and its values, which were the material for Persius's satires.

It is generally recognized that Persius does not have the qualities that have guaranteed the continuing popularity of Horace and Juvenal. Yet even his positive qualities have been undervalued in recent centuries and his originality has been denied. It has often been said that he is a mere imitator of Lucilius and Horace. This generalization fails to appreciate the nature of emulation (*aemulatio*) in Latin literature, and in this study an attempt is made to show how far Persius built upon his predecessors' work, going beyond imitation to the creation of poetry that can rightly claim to be original. The focus in the second chapter is upon the satiric tradition, but the nature of Persius's emulation is an important feature also of the third, fourth, and fifth chapters, in which the satires are analyzed individually. In these chapters Persius is allowed as far as possible to speak for himself, and the discussion aims to illuminate for the reader the satiric and poetic qualities of Persius's work. His two greatest

satires, the first and fifth, have been extensively
dealt with in recent scholarship, but the present study
takes a more sympathetic view than has been the case
with many of Persius's commentators. It aims in particular at a lucid exposition of the immensely complex
first satire, which has a perceptible structure and
coherence.

The comparatively slight second satire was admired
and frequently quoted by Christian apologists, yet it
has been generally disregarded in modern times, largely
because of the overwhelming influence of Juvenal's
tenth satire and Dr. Johnson's imitation, The Vanity
of Human Wishes. Since Juvenal was writing on a completely different scale (his poem is five times the
length of Persius's), a comparison is not very meaningful. It is to the point, however, to examine Persius's
second satire both for its own qualities and as the
starting-point for Juvenal. The third satire is devoted to the central theme of Persius's poems, moral
training for the good life. Its concern is the education of the will, and at its end the philosopher,
appearing as a doctor examining his patient (that is,
the young student), establishes the healthy standard of
virtue. This theme is continued in the fourth satire,
where the student is a candidate for public office.
The philosopher (at first in the persona of Socrates,
later speaking through the mask of the satirist) shows
that self-knowledge is a necessary prerequisite for
virtue, most especially in one who aspires to take an
active part in politics. The second, third, and fourth
satires are connected, with the weighty third satire
balanced by the two lesser poems that flank it. They
lead naturally to the massive fifth satire, to which
(along with the sixth) the fifth chapter is devoted.
In it Persius relates his own education under Cornutus
to the general principles discussed in satires 2-4. As
the climax of his book, the satirist shows that only
through training in philosophy can one achieve true
freedom. It remains only for Persius to add a kind of
epilogue in the sixth satire. It is cast in the form
of an Horatian epistle addressed to the lyric poet
Caesius Bassus. Its tone is relaxed and genial com-
pared with that of its more didactic predecessors (satires 2-5), and it provides an appropriate conclusion
to Persius's book.

After the survey of the satires contained in chapters 3-5, the sixth chapter of this study is devoted to a discussion of the style of Persius, which has been unduly (and generally uncritically) emphasized in adverse judgments of his poetry. The chapter includes material for the most part available only in comparatively inaccessible journals, and there is more attention to details of vocabulary, diction, and metaphorical writing, than is to be found in most earlier studies. There is no comparable discussion in English. This chapter aims to help the reader understand the nature of Persius's poetic and satiric techniques. Inevitably the chapter is more technical than the others, but it has also been written with the reader in mind who can approach Persius only though the medium of translation. This same reader, however, is assumed to be one who appreciates the indirect workings of the true poet's mind, and it accepts without apology that good poetry will invariably require an intellectual effort. It does not make a virtue of obscurity, but it does seek out the reasons for the poet's preferring a difficult form of expression to one whose meanings lie close to the surface.

The seventh and final chapter is a brief review of Persius's fortunes since the posthumous publication of his poems. Again, this chapter contains much material that is only available to the diligent scholar working in a research library. It has been written from the point of view of one who appreciates the European tradition of classical satire. While specialists in Donne, Boileau, Dryden, or Pope will no doubt be disappointed that more has not been said about these authors, enough has been said, it is hoped, to encourage nonspecialist readers to pursue their own lines of enquiry. Above all, the chapter shows how influential Persius in fact was for 1,600 years, and it guides the reader to further exploration or, at the least, to a just assessment of Persius's importance.

It remains finally to say something about recent scholarship on Persius. Despite the low state of his fortunes he has generated an immense amount of commentary, including two recent commentaries in English, the first since 1893. The two recent full-length studies in English, those by Dessen and Bramble, are unsuitable as introductions to Persius for the readers for whom this book is written. By far the greatest amount of work on Persius has been done in Italy, Germany, and France, and there has been no choice but to include the more significant non-English publications in the bibliography, where they have a larger proportion of space than is usual for books in this series. The English reader is better served by his translators, for the translations of Merwin and Rudd are both good companions on the voyage of exploration of Persius's satire. Readers are urged to read the satires themselves, whether in Latin or in translation, as they read this book. Then the chief goal of the book will have been achieved, to let Persius himself speak to a modern audience.

Mark Morford

The Ohio State University

Acknowledgments

This book has been written over a period when heavy administrative responsibilities made continuous research difficult. I am especially grateful to two colleagues, Professors Charles Babcock and Geoffrey Woodhead, who made possible the two periods of uninterrupted time that allowed me to do the basic research. Professor Woodhead encouraged me to spend a term as Visiting Scholar in Residence at Corpus Christi College, Cambridge, and was my genial host and generous colleague there. Professor Babcock kindly undertook my duties at Columbus during my absence, and later as departmental chairman supported my request for a term of assigned research duty. To him and to the former dean of the College of Humanities at the Ohio State University, Diether Haenicke, I am most grateful.

Much of the secondary literature on Persius, like the early printed editions, is hard to come by, and I owe a special debt to the staffs of several libraries. In particular I am grateful to the staffs of the library of the University of Cambridge, of the library of the Cambridge Faculty of Classics, and of the Houghton Library of Harvard University. I have been generously served by the staff of the library at the Ohio State University, and I owe particular thanks to Mrs. Clara Goldslager, of the Office of Interlibrary Loan Services, for her cheerful, kindly, and efficient help over many months.

I am grateful to Mr. W. H. Bond, librarian of the Houghton Library of Harvard University, for permission to reproduce an illustration from an incunabulum in the Houghton Library as the frontispiece to this book; to Messrs. Faber and Faber, Ltd., of London, and New Directions Publishing Corporation, of New York, for permission to quote from <u>The Literary Essays of Ezra Pound</u>, copyright 1935 by Ezra Pound.

Mrs. Karen Givler has helped me immeasurably by typing the final draft and considerable portions of an earlier one; my thanks also are due to Mrs. Jimmye

Wheatley and Ms. Christine Pignatiello, who also undertook extensive typing from a manuscript full of idio-
syncrasies. The kind and cheerful cooperation of these
three members of the staff of the Department of Classics has made the writing of this book far more of a
pleasure.

The typescript of this book was submitted to the
publishers in November 1980. Within a few months the
commentaries of Jenkinson and Harvey appeared. It has
been neither possible nor necessary to make extensive
revisions in the light of these two works. I have been
content to add references to them for certain disputed
passages in the chapters on the satires and style of
Persius, and I have made appropriate additions to the
notes and bibliography. I am grateful to the publishers for the opportunity of making these adjustments.

It was the enthusiasm and encouragement of Professor
Philip Levine, general editor of the Latin authors in
this series, that led to my undertaking the book, and
for this I shall always be grateful. Finally, I acknowledge my greatest debt of all, which is to the
patient understanding and never-failing encouragement
of Martha, my wife.

Chronology

ca. 125 B.C.   Lucilius writing satire.

35   First book of Horace's _Satires_ published.

30   Second book of Horace's _Satires_.

8   Horace dies.

34 A.D.   December, Persius born.

49   Seneca returns from exile to tutor Nero.

ca. 50   Persius begins studies with Cornutus.

54   Nero becomes emperor.

59   Murder of Agrippina, Nero's mother. Decline of Seneca's influence.

62   November, Persius dies. His satires published posthumously.

Seneca retires from court.

64   July, great fire at Rome.

65   April, failure of Pisonian Conspiracy against Nero. Seneca and Lucan executed.

66   Thrasea and Petronius executed.

68   June, Nero dies.

ca. 105   First book of Juvenal's satires published.

ca. 130   Juvenal dies.

1605   Isaac Casaubon's edition of Persius.

1693   Dryden's _Discourse on Satire_.

Abbreviations

C.J.	Classical Journal
C.Q.	Classical Quarterly
C.R.	Classical Review
F.P.L.	Fragmenta Poetarum Latinorum. Edited by W. Morel. Leipzig: Teubner, 1927
O.C.T.	Oxford Classical Texts
R.-E.	Pauly-Wissowa-Kroll. Real-Enclyclopädie der klassischen Altertumswissenschaft. Stuttgart: Druckenmuller, 1893-1980
R.O.L.	Remains of Old Latin. Edited and translated by E. H. Warmington. 4 vols. London: Heinemann; Cambridge: Harvard University Press, 1935-59
Rostock	W. Krenkel, ed., Römische Satire. Wissenschaftliche Zeitschrift der Universität Rostock, Gesellschaft- und Sprachwissenschaftliche Reihe, 15. Rostock, 1966.
R.S.C.	Rivista di Studi Classici
T.A.P.A.	Transactions of the American Philological Association
Volterra Scritti	Scritti per il xix Centenario della Nascita di Persio. Biblioteca della Rassegna Volterrana, no. 3. Volterra: Accademia dei Sepolti, 1936

Metrical abbreviations

u -   indicates a short syllable followed by a long one:
        this combination forms an iamb.

- -   indicates two long syllables: this combination
        forms a spondee.

- u u   indicates a long syllable followed by two short
        syllables: this combination forms a dactyl.

Chapter One
Life, Background, Literary and Social Milieu
Life and Friends

Ancient poets were careful not to reveal too much of their personal biography and this is especially so with Roman satirists. The satirist adopted a persona or mask through which he addressed his audience, which might vary from satire to satire. Even the most vivid scenes cannot be taken as autobiographical, nor can particular attitudes adopted by the persona be said necessarily to reveal the author's own views. Horace tells us that Lucilius, the first of the four great Roman hexameter satirists, "entrusted his secret thoughts to his books, as though to friends he trusted . . . so that his whole life, when he was an old man, was displayed like a . . . painting" [Satire 2.1.30-34]. This, if true, was exceptional, and certainly the case of Persius is quite different. Only in the fifth satire, when he tells of his debt to his teacher Cornutus [Satire 5.21-51], can we be sure that he is revealing the actual facts of his life. Our main source for his life is in fact an ancient Vita (Life) which several manuscripts attribute to Valerius Probus, a grammarian, editor, and literary critic from Beirut, who worked in the later part of the first century. Its true authorship cannot be established, but it appears to go back to a time close to Persius's own and so gives us more reliable information than we normally can glean from such Lives.

Aules Persius Flaccus was born on 4 December 34 at Volaterrae (modern Volterra) and died of a stomach disease shortly before his twenty-eighth birthday, on his own property a few miles from Rome, on 24 November 62. Volaterrae is an Etruscan town and the name Aules is an Etruscan form of the Roman name Aulus. Although the Etruscans had long since lost their power and any political identity separate from Rome, people were proud to boast of their Etruscan descent. Persius himself refers to it at Satire 3.28-29, and Horace

1

refers several times to the Etruscan lineage of his patron, Maecenas, whom in the very first line of his Odes he addresses as "Maecenas, descendant of kings." Persius's Etruscan descent associated him with much that was finest and most ancient in Rome's cultural and social traditions, so that as a satirist he could claim to criticize the leaders of Roman society as one of their peers. This attribute he shared with Lucilius (ca. 168-102 B.C.), whose family had senatorial connections and was affluent. Horace (65-8 B.C.) and Juvenal (ca. 60-130), on the other hand, criticized the Roman aristocracy as outsiders. Horace was the son of a freedman (that is, his father had once been a slave) and owed his position to his education and ability, which brought him the friendship and trust of Maecenas, the great minister of Augustus. There is hardly any reliable evidence for Juvenal's social circumstances, but he writes as an outsider whose exclusion from the respectable circles of Roman society fueled the fires of satiric bitterness (or, as he himself called it, indignatio).

Persius was an eques ("knight"), that is, a member of the propertied class, and the Life says that he left an estate of two million sesterces to his mother and sister, separate, it would seem, from the real-estate, books, and silver that are also mentioned in the Life. Thus he was comparable in wealth to a modern millionaire, and his comfortable situation has some bearing on the facts that his satires deal with a narrower range of Roman life than those of Horace and display more detachment than the vigorous anger of Juvenal. His life was uneventful. Free from involvement in public life he lived, it seems, devoted to his mother, sister, and aunt, and was chaste and moderate in his personal habits. His father died when he was about six and his mother, Fulvia Sisennia (her name is Etruscan), married as her second husband a well-to-do eques called Fusius, who also died prematurely.

This sheltered existence, dominated by women, would hardly provide the raw material for satire, and the Life is informative about the people who influenced Persius's thinking. After completing his elementary education at Volaterrae he continued his secondary education at Rome, where among his teachers were the famous grammarian Remmius Palaemon and the rhetorician Verginius Flavus. Remmius may have been the teacher of Quintilian, the most distinguished professor of education in first-century Rome. A freedman, conceited, arrogant, and luxury-loving, Remmius was nevertheless influential as a scholar and literary critic. In particular he taught that the Augustan poets, especially Vergil and Horace, should be considered as the true classical models, rather than their predecessors such as Ennius. Second, he was exact in his use of words (distinguishing, for example, between the two Latin words for "drop," stilla and gutta). In the next century Juvenal [Satire 6.451-53] criticized the pedantic blue-stocking who used Remmius's Art of Grammar as the canon of correct speaking by which to correct her husband. The two features of Remmius's teaching are easily traced in the work of Persius, most especially in the first Satire.

Verginius Flavus was a popular teacher of rhetoric, whose work was admired and quoted by Quintilian. Tacitus [Annals 15.71] records his exile by Nero in 65, linking him in this with the foremost Stoic teacher of the time, Musonius Rufus.

Grammar (which included literary theory and criticism), rhetoric, and philosophy were the substance of a liberal Roman education, and all three branches were combined in the person who had the most enduring influence upon Persius, Annaeus Cornutus, whose friend Persius became when he was sixteen. The relationship was not formal, like that of a student and classroom teacher, for it was rather the relaxed association of philosopher and disciple. The friendship lasted for the rest of Persius's life, and Cornutus (along with Caesius Bassus, mentioned below) edited the Satires for posthumous publication, while he advised Fulvia (Persius's mother) to suppress her son's other works. He was also a beneficiary of Persius's will.

Persius himself tells us a great deal about his debt to Cornutus in the fifth satire, especially lines 21-52, which we shall discuss later. Cornutus was a freedman, a native of Leptis in Africa, and his name, Annaeus, implies that he had been a slave in the family that included Seneca and Lucan among its members. He too was a successful teacher, a rhetorician, a prolific writer, and author of a commentary on Vergil. Above all, he was a Stoic philosopher, whose teaching, Persius tells us, formed his own morals at the crossroads of adolescence [Satire 5.30-40]. He was also a

demanding critic of Persius's poetry [Satire 5.5-29].
Like Verginius and Musonius, he was exiled by Nero in
65.
     These three scholars--Remmius, Verginius, and Cornu-
tus--were the most important influences upon Persius.
To them can be traced his precise use of words and
collocations of words and metaphors; his close knowledge of the literary tradition (especially in epic and
satire); finally, his Stoic philosophy.
     The Life mentions other friends in the circle of
Persius. In early adolescence he formed a lifelong
friendship with Caesius Bassus, the only Roman lyric
poet other than Horace to be mentioned by name in
Quintilian's summary of Roman literature [Institutio
Oratoria 10.1.96], although without enthusiasm. Persius, who addressed the sixth satire to Bassus, is more
complimentary [Satire 6.1-6] in his admiration of
Bassus's skill as a lyric poet. He was much older than
Persius, who calls him senex ("old man"), and was said
to have died in the eruption of Vesuvius in 79. He
wrote a treatise on metrics and so may have had some
influence on Persius's versification.
     Five years younger than Persius was Lucan (39-65),
the greatest poetic genius of the age and author of the
unfinished epic on the Civil War between Caesar and
Pompey. The Life says that Persius came to know Lucan
when both were students of Cornutus. The story is
probably apocryphal that Lucan applauded Persius as he
was reciting, saying, "You are composing real poetry:
mine is just trifling." Such modesty is not typical of
Lucan, even before he came to write his epic, and it is
doubtful that the two young poets formed a continuous
friendship. Lucan's brilliant gifts and his ambition
(helped by his relationship to Seneca, Nero's tutor and
later principal minister) led him to embark on a public
career, which ended very probably in 62, the year of
Persius's death. Three years later he himself perished
in the purge of 65. Lucan shared with Persius a love
of liberty, expressed with greater passion than Persius
could muster in the fifth satire, and a devotion to
Stoic philosophy.
     We have mentioned Seneca (4-65), the leading author
of the age and a dominant influence in politics and
literature during the first five years of Nero's reign
(54-59), who retired from the court in 62 and, like his
nephew, Lucan, was forced to commit suicide in 65.

Persius did not like him: "He also came to know Seneca late, but not so as to be attracted by his intellect," says the *Life*. A similar skepticism is expressed at greater length by Quintilian [10.1.125-31], who particularly disliked Seneca's egoism and what he thought was the pernicious influence on the young of his facile rhetorical style. Quintilian believed strongly in the close relationship of morality and rhetoric, and the same belief underlies much of Persius's first satire. It is likely, too, that the rather relaxed Stoicism of Seneca had compromised with worldly standards too much for the more doctrinaire Persius. Seneca was wealthy and politically powerful, and the austere period of his life when he both practiced the Stoic maxim of "living according to Nature" and wrote his *Letters to Lucilius* occurred after Persius's death. Persius's rejection of Seneca is significant as evidence for his independence from contemporary literary fashion (the subject of the first satire) and for his uncompromising acceptance of Stoic principles.

The *Life* mentions four older friends with whom Persius had a close emotional involvement, namely, Servilius, Agathinus, Petronius, and Paetus. Servilius Nonianus, whom he looked upon "as father," had been consul in 35 and died in 59. He was an historian of some gifts, although too diffuse according to Quintilian [10.1.102]. The other three older friends were in the circle of Cornutus. Two of them were apparently doctors, Agathinus (or Agathemerus), a Spartan, and Petronius Aristocrates, from Asia Minor, and are described in the *Life* as men who in their way of life were "most learned and pure." Both men are quoted by Galen: the former was the author of a work *De Helleboro* (on madness and its cure, perhaps), the latter is called *grammaticus* (perhaps meaning "scholar"). Both were enthusiastic students of philosophy, and the frequent use of medical metaphors by Persius may be due to these friendships.

Another older friend, not mentioned in the *Life*, was Plotius Macrinus, the addressee of Persius's second satire. The scholiast, (that is, ancient commentator) says that he also had been a student in the house of Servilius, and it is implied that he was older than Persius whom "he loved with a father's feelings." Persius was further said to have bought some land from him on favorable terms.

The fourth older friend mentioned in the Life was
the most important. Paetus Thrasea, who for ten years
was Persius's close friend, was married to Arria, a
relative of Persius and the daughter of the famous
heroine, Arria (the Elder), whose dying words in 42,
"Paetus, it doesn't hurt," encouraged her husband to
follow her in suicide. Thrasea was consul in 56, and
for some years he attempted to reconcile his uncompromising belief in liberty with the rule of Nero. By
59 he could no longer accept the increasingly murderous
autocracy of Nero, and in 63 he gave up attending the
Senate. Although he avoided involvement in the
Pisonian conspiracy of 65 he was forced by Nero to
commit suicide in 66. Thrasea was the leading figure
among the aristocrats opposed on principle to Nero. As
the biographer and philosophical successor of Cato the
Younger he had an unshakeable belief in liberty, as
defined by the Stoics, and it led him and his friends,
themselves Stoics, to put their principles above their
personal security (1). Persius's association with
such a man for ten years must have been of the greatest
importance to the development of his thought and especially of his independence as a satirist. Through him
he had contact with the higher levels of Roman politics
and learned the practical meaning of liberty in a
context different from the theoretical one of literary
and philosophical discussions. Yet it must also be
admitted that Persius uses libertas (for example, in
Satire 5.73) generally in the nonpolitical sense,
basing himself upon the Stoic paradox, "only the wise
are free."
     It is sometimes assumed that Persius was a recluse
"who must have formed his notions of life as much from
books as from experience" (2), living a sheltered life
and surrounded by attentive female relatives. The
evidence does not support this view. He traveled
abroad with Thrasea on more than one occasion, and the
range of his friendships shows clearly that he was
associated with men who led active lives (two of them
rose to be consul, still a distinguished achievement
even under the Empire) and pondered deeply on the
ethical problems posed by political developments in the
reign of Nero. Persius's personal involvement in
public life was admittedly less than that of his predecessors in satire, for Lucilius had participated in
the Spanish campaigns of his friend and patron, Scipio

Aemilianus, while Horace, who had fought on the Republican side at the battle of Philippi, was the friend of Maecenas, Augustus's minister, and declined a pressing invitation to serve as secretary to Augustus himself. But times had changed from those of Lucilius and Horace, for all the literary men of Nero's time who had been the emperor's friends and associates--Lucan, Seneca, and Petronius--were forced to commit suicide. Satire was at best a dangerous pursuit under an autocracy, and independence, essential for a poet, was especially a necessity for the satirist. The intense and private quality of Persius's satire is due more to his chosen way of writing than to lack of personal observation. His range of subject matter is narrower than that of Lucilius, Horace, and Juvenal, and reflects the preoccupation with ethics that characterized the Stoic thought of the age. But his own genius, and the friendship of men such as Cornutus and Thrasea, ensured that his satire would be incisive and vital.

The Neronian Age

Persius's maturity began with the introduction to Cornutus, when he was sixteen years old, four years before the start of Nero's reign (54-68). The Neronian cultural, social, and political background is therefore relevant to the work of a satirist who criticized the literature and morals of the age.

Nero was the first emperor to come to the throne after an education designed with his succession as the goal. His mother, Agrippina the Younger, married her uncle, the emperor Claudius, in 49 after the disgrace and execution of his former wife. She was driven by consuming ambition for power. With the aid of Seneca, to whom Nero's education was entrusted, and Burrus, prefect of the Praetorian Guard, she prepared the way for Nero. He displaced Claudius's own son Britannicus as the heir-apparent and was betrothed to Octavia, the emperor's daughter. When Claudius was murdered in October 54, the succession was smoothly managed, and the seventeen-year-old emperor was quickly accepted by army and people. The reign began well. Nero's public pronouncememts, written for him by Seneca, promised a return to constitutional government and the consistent administration of law, and even the murder of Britanni-

cus in 55 did not shake his position. Abroad, the
campaigns of Corbulo in the east provided victories
enough for Roman glory.

Culturally the new reign was to represent a renaissance of literature and the arts, fields in which Nero
had a deep interest and some ability. It was to be
politically and culturally a new Augustan age, and
Nero, so the court-poets wrote, was a new Apollo on
earth to preside over the Golden Age of Roman culture.
It is true that the reign did witness a remarkable
flourishing of literature, drama, architecture, music,
and painting, the more striking for its contrast with
the culturally barren reigns of Tiberius, Gaius, and
Claudius (3). In literature Seneca created virtually a
new prose style in his voluminous philosophical
writings and revived tragedy with his dramas. His
nephew Lucan re-created and transformed Vergilian epic,
while a minor poet, Calpurnius Siculus (who was not
close to the emperor), revived pastoral poetry with his
Eclogues. Varronian satire (that is, mixed prose and
verse with diverse subject matter) was revived in the
Apocolocyntosis of Seneca early in the reign and later
in the infinitely greater novel of Petronius, the
Satyricon. In architecture and painting the Golden
House of Nero was preeminent, and its use of brick-
faced concrete and its frescoes had lasting influence
in the history of European art and architecture. We
cannot be so specific about music, but there is no
doubt about the personal involvement of Nero in musical
performances, and his encouragement led to the establishment of "Games" on the Greek model, that is, festivals where poetic, dramatic, and musical performances
were prominent.

Such activities, however, could hardly govern an
empire, and Nero's own character, joined to his lack of
experience in military and political affairs, made
deterioration inevitable. In 59 he instigated the
murder of his mother, and from that time the influence
of Seneca and Burrus declined, while others promised
the independence that had been denied him in the years
of his tutelage. This stage of the reign ended in 62
with the death of Burrus, the retirement of Seneca, the
rejection and murder of Octavia, and, finally, Nero's
marriage with Poppaea, the beautiful, talented, and
unprincipled former wife of Otho (who was himself to be
emperor for a short time in 69). It was also marked by

the celebration of the Juvenalia in 59, the first of
the musical and dramatic festivals inaugurated by Nero
and undoubtedly a stimulus to cultural activity. This
festival was followed by the Neronia in 60.

These were the circumstances of the society that
Persius criticized. The literary renaissance meant new
literary styles, and changes in literary taste are
among the targets of Persius's first satire. The
deliberate cultivation of artistic and literary activities among the governing classes, and especially in
Nero's circle of associates, was a challenge to the
traditional values of the Roman upper class. For centuries there had been cultivated aristocrats, men like
Scipio Africanus who welcomed the superior cultural
heritage of Hellenistic civilization, or Julius Caesar,
who was able to meet the leading writers and orators of
the day as an equal. For these men cultural pursuits
were separate from their public life, and military and
political affairs were their primary activities. To
secure the greatness of Rome and achieve personal glory
were the ideals of the Roman aristocracy in the late
Republic and early Empire. Nero had had no military
experience, and his personal character combined with
his education to lead him to attempt to change the
traditional priorities. So long as the state was well
governed by his subordinates such a policy could have
been comparatively harmless, however much it aroused
the scorn and resentment of conservative aristocrats.
What in fact happened was far worse, the result of
Nero's self-indulgence, natural disasters (notably the
great fire at Rome of 64), and failures abroad, especially in Britain, Judaea, and Armenia.

Seneca and Burrus were replaced in 62 as Nero's
advisers by Tigellinus, one of the new Praetorian pre-
fects, and Poppaea, now Nero's wife. From 62 Nero's
enthusiasm for musical and dramatic pursuits was publicly indulged, culminating in the seventeen-month tour
of Greece in 66-68 from which he returned with 1,808
crowns, prizes won in musical contests. His egoism
encouraged the development of autocracy, as opposed to
the system of power shared between the emperor and the
aristocracy that Augustus had introduced. Those who
opposed Nero, or were thought to be a threat to his
preeminence, were exiled or executed (usually by man-
dated suicide), and the economic resources of the
Empire were increasingly squandered to provide for the

extravagances of the emperor and his court. His own position was weakened by the fire that destroyed nearly one third and damaged much of the rest of Rome in July 64, and he gave more ammunition to his critics by appropriating a large part of the center of the city for his new complex of palaces, villas, parks, and gardens, which we know as the Golden House (4). In 66 his egomania reached its climax in the "Golden Day" at which the Armenian King, Tiridates, did obeisance to Nero. Public spectacles, however, and aesthetic triumphs could not long defer the collapse of the regime. Nero had survived a major conspiracy in 65, largely thanks to the conspirators' own nervousness (5), but in 68 dissatisfaction among the upper classes at Rome and a revolt in Gaul ensured Nero's downfall. He was declared a public enemy, and on 9 June he committed suicide: he was thirty years old (6).

Roman Stoicism

Although Persius died in 62, the developments of the last six years of the reign were already clearly foreshadowed. One reaction of the educated upper class to the excesses of Nero was to turn to philosophy, for the most part to Stoicism. Roman Stoicism of the period combined the ideal of simplicity of life (lived "according to Nature") with service to the state and one's fellow man (7). At the same time it emphasized the dignity of the individual and therefore made liberty a central theme. If political liberty were curtailed, for example under a tyranny, personal liberty could still be asserted: a man need not compromise his Stoic principles, and the ultimate expression of individual liberty was suicide. This austere ethical teaching drew its strength from the basic Stoic doctrine that physical and temporal goods, such as wealth, health, and comfort, are "indifferent"--that is, they cannot affect the things that are primarily important to a human being, above all, virtue. Therefore Roman Stoicism had an overwhelmingly moral emphasis, teaching that virtue was more important than physical and temporal benefits, and that passions, such as anger and fear, were to be suppressed. Many Stoics were interested also in scientific questions and developed theories about physics, natural history, and cosmology.

These appear prominently in Seneca and Lucan, but not at all in Persius.

For Thrasea and other Stoics in public life the reign of Nero posed acute ethical dilemmas. Some, like Seneca, were able to compromise, but others, like Thrasea, could not. The phrase "Stoic opposition" is often used of the men opposed to Nero, but it should be used cautiously. The Stoics were not necessarily Republicans. Thrasea himself, for example, had as a senator and consul taken an active part in the government until 62, like other prominent Stoics. The leading Stoic teacher of the time, Musonius Rufus, wrote his treatise <u>That Kings Should Study Philosophy</u> upon the premise that monarchy is not an evil. The leaders of the Pisonian conspiracy in 65 did not seek to abolish the principate but to replace Nero by a better emperor. Yet when it became obvious that the principate and liberty could not be reconciled, the Stoics knew where their priorities lay. They followed the example of the younger Cato, who a century before had chosen suicide rather than surrender to Julius Caesar. They affirmed their liberty by refusal to compromise, which led in many cases to exile or death. For example, one of the charges against Thrasea in 66 was that he "made a show of liberty in order to subvert the principate" (8).

Thus Stoics in the time of Nero were deeply concerned with ethical and political questions. Persius died before the dilemma of the Stoics became acute, but we know, from the writings of Seneca and the accounts of the reaction at Rome to the murder of Agrippina, that thoughtful people were already facing the problems. Since Persius was not involved in public life he had no inducement to write political satire, although he hints at the possibility in the first satire [lines 107-21]. In any case to have done so would have invited his own destruction and that of his works. Tacitus and Suetonius record examples of authors who were executed and their works burned because they openly attacked the vices of an emperor or, equally serious, were thought to have done so. Therefore Persius directed his Stoic doctrines to the ethical side of Roman society. Thus in the first satire he explored the connection between morality and literature; in the fourth between self-knowledge and honesty in public life. In the fifth satire he examines liberty, but in the context of personal morality. And so it is with

the other satires, in which he deals with standard
moral themes and exhorts his hearers to follow the
precepts of philosophy. His satire criticizes universal faults in human nature; we will not find in them
attacks on contemporary political leaders. Yet we
would be wrong to dismiss them as irrelevant to Roman
society in the Neronian age. The moral, cultural, and
political developments that we have outlined were not
unobserved by the satirist. In his satires we have
authentic criticism of the moral trends of the age.

Chapter Two
Persius and the Satiric Tradition

Introduction

Roman authors were acutely conscious of the tradition of the particular genre in which they were writing. From the Greeks the Romans inherited the concept of to prepon ("what is fitting"), which finds its most memorable expression in Horace's Art of Poetry. Horace opens his third and final apologia for his satires [Satire 2.1] by quoting the charge that he has "stretched his work beyond the laws of satire" ("ultra legem tendere opus"). Satirists were as concerned as other poets with their place in the tradition and the relationship of their work to that of their predecessors. This is not merely literary narcissism, for such considerations led the satirist to say a good deal about the scope, content, and purpose of his poetry. While it was important to acknowledge one's debt to earlier writers--explicitly or by direct quotation or adaptation--it was equally important for the poet to tell his audience how he was altering the inherited tradition and why his predecessors' satire was inadequate for his own purposes. Such an approach is typically Roman: indeed, satire was thought to be the only exclusively Roman literary genre (1) (as opposed to a Roman adaptation of a Greek genre), and its major writers show the Roman characteristics of respect for tradition combined with adaptability to changing circumstances.

The origins of satire, like the derivation of the word satura, are a matter for debate, and we need not enter into the controversy here (2). The most likely explanation is that satura takes its name from lanx satura, that is, a dish (lanx) full (satura) of various first fruits offered to the gods. Thus variety was from the beginning a feature of Roman satire, and long after its form and content had become stabilized the last of the Roman satirists, Juvenal (ca. 55-130) described his satire as farrago ("a medley"). His summary is a neat statement of the scope of satire [Juvenal, Satire 1.85-86]: "Whatever men do--their prayers, fear, anger, pleasure, happiness, business-- all makes up the medley of my book."

As a literary form satire developed in two directions. The earliest Latin author to gather into a book a miscellaneous collection of poetry in different meters and on various subjects was Ennius (239-169 B.C.), the author also of the Annales, the first great Roman national epic. Neither Horace nor Persius nor Juvenal mentions his Saturae (as he called his collection), and it is Lucilius, not Ennius, that they considered to be the founder of the satiric tradition. This is because Ennius's Saturae were not in their view part of the tradition of hexameter satire in which they wrote. His medley of meters and subjects was continued in the other satiric tradition, of which Varro (116-27 B.C.), was the leading exponent, and it was further developed in the reign of Nero by Seneca and Petronius (3). This type of satire is called Menippean, from Varro's Greek model, Mennippus (ca. 250 B.C.). Its distinctive features were a prose narrative with verse interludes in various meters, forming a loosely structured whole, as varied in content as in form.

The other satiric tradition is the one that concerns us, and its founder was Lucilius (4), a Roman knight who lived ca. 168-102 B.C. His whole poetic activity was devoted to satire, and Horace, Persius, and Juvenal were right to look to him as the founder of their genre. Like Ennius he began by writing in a mixture of meters (books 26-29 contain iambics of different systems and hexameters), but with book 30 he turned exclusively to hexameters and in so doing definitely set the tradition of the hexameter satirists. In books 1-21 (which are later than books 26-30) he wrote only hexameters. Only about 1,400 lines survive, very few fragments being more than one or two lines long, so that it is difficult for us to assess his achievement. Many of the fragments survive in quotations by grammarians, for example, illustrating unusual words or usages, and give an uneven idea of Lucilius's work. Yet the surviving fragments, combined with the judgments of later authors (especially Horace and Persius) allow us to give a fairly detailed picture of the tradition that he founded. Before doing so, however, we should consider what he inherited from Greek writers.

The Greek Tradition

We should immediately distinguish between the genre of satura and the satiric spirit. When Quintilian claimed that "satire is wholly Roman" [10.1.93], he was thinking of the former. The Greeks, whom the Romans followed in every other literary genre (with the possible exception of letter writing), did not write satires as such. On the other hand, they wrote a great deal that was satirical, and the Roman satirists freely acknowledged their debt to the Greek tradition. Horace, for example, opens his first literary apologia [Satire 1.4.1] with the names of the three masters of Greek Old Comedy of the fifth century, in a resonant hexameter, "Eupolis atque Cratinus Aristophanesque poetae," and he neatly summarizes Lucilius's debt to them [1.4.3-6]: "if anyone deserved to be marked out as a criminal or thief, or because he was an adulterer or cut-throat or notorious in some other way, him they would freely and publicly criticize. From them Lucilius totally derives. . . ." So Persius at the end of his program-satire [1.123-26] makes the same appeal to justify his excoriating the vices of society: "You, who are inspired by outspoken Cratinus or grow pale poring over angry Eupolis with the other Grand Old Man [that is, Aristophanes], look also at my words, if you are prepared to listen to something that is more than froth. Let my reader come from them with well-steamed ear." While no comparable fragment survives from Lucilius, it is at least probable that he acknowledged the same debt. At any rate, Horace and Persius make clear that a primary function of satire was a part of the tradition inherited from Greece, that is, social and moral criticism. It is in the so-called Old Comedy of Athens that such criticism was freely offered, indirectly through the action and dialogue, directly in the parabasis, a monologue in which the poet spoke to his audience through the medium of the Chorus.

A second vehicle for Greek moral and social criticism was the informal discourses of popular philosophers, who were especially a feature of city life in the Hellenistic age (that is, between 323 and 146 B.C.) (5). These teachers did not as a rule adhere to any one system of philosophy, although they were often closest to the Cynics, the least dogmatic of the Hellenistic schools of philosophy, and their diatribes (as

their discourses are technically known) were delivered
at street corners or at any other place where a knot of
hearers could be gathered (6). The informal nature of
the diatribe is better expressed by the Latin word
sermones (meaning "conversations" or "talks"), the very
word, in fact, that Horace used for the title of his
satires. Horace mentions the best-known of these Hellenistic philosophers, Bion, a native of the Crimea,
who lived at Athens in the first half of the third
century B.C. (he died ca. 255). He is described in
more detail by Diogenes Laertius, the compiler of a set
of Lives of the Philosophers during the first century
A.D. (7). Horace refers to Bion's "black wit," and
Diogenes amplifies the caustic nature of Bion's criticism in emphasizing his lack of manners and principles
and his atheism. Above all, his teaching was unsystem-
atic, and the informal structure of Roman hexameter
satire certainly owes something to this aspect of the
diatribe. Bion was unconventional: his discourses
were enlivened by epigrams (called by the Romans sen-
tentiae and a particularly prominent feature in the
writing of Persius's contemporaries), parody (especially of epic), rhyme, and verbal jingles. In style he
favored metaphors drawn from everyday activities or
from medicine, sometimes used merely to illustrate an
ethical point, sometimes so developed as to take over
the abstract idea that they were introduced to illustrate. From another Hellenistic philosopher, the Cynic
Teles (ca. 235 B.C.), we know that Bion personified the
virtues and vices, for example, by having Poverty make
a speech on the virtues of self-sufficiency. Persius
adopted this technique in his fifth satire with the
dramatic presentation of Avarice and Luxury [Satire
5.132-56].
    Here are some examples from Bion's diatribes. "Old
Age is the haven from [the sea of] troubles"; "wealth
is the sinews of success"; "do not try to change things
but, like sailors, adapt yourself to circumstances";
"in prosperity crowd on full sail, in adversity reef
your sail"; "marry an ugly wife and trouble's in store;
marry a pretty one, she'll be a whore" (an approximation to the jingle in the Greek of poinên and koinên).
Other features of the Hellenistic diatribe were the
dialogue, through the introduction of an imaginary
interlocutor (Persius engagingly reveals this device in
his first satire, line 44, "whoever you are whom I have

just introduced as an adversary"), and the use of animal fables, of which Horace's story of the two mice is a brilliant Roman adaptation [Satire 2.6.79-117].

A third genre through which the Greek satiric spirit influenced Roman satire was the iambic, poems of short to moderate length containing political, social, and moral criticism, often expressed in bitter terms and with scathing attacks on individuals. Its greatest exponent was also one of the earliest, Archilochus of Lesbos (ca. 620 B.C.), who was the direct inspiration of Horace's earliest published poetry, the Epodes (ca. 42-35 B.C.). Satirical iambics were revived in the Hellenistic age, especially by the Alexandrian poet Callimachus (ca. 275 B.C.) (8). One variation of the iambic meter was the choliambic or scazon (that is, "limping" iambic), in which the trimeter (that is, a line formed of three double iambs) ended with a spondee (--) instead of an iamb (u-, a short syllable followed by a long one). The effect is to slow up the progress of the line to its end, so that it appears to limp. For example, the first scazon of Persius's prologue reads nēc fóntĕ lábră prólŭĭ căbállīnō, and the reader who reads the last two syllables if they were -ĭnō will quickly see the differences in the rhythm. The inventor of scazons was Hipponax (ca. 540 B.C.), and in the first line of his iambics Callimachus describes himself as if he were a resurrected Hipponax. Another Hellenistic choliambic poet was Phoenix of Colophon (ca. 280 B.C.) (9), whose choliambics often had a strong gnomic element (that is, expressing general maxims in proverbial or epigrammatic form), combined with a tendency to moralize. The following quotation from an anonymous choliambic poem attacking greed is illustrative: "Well, I would prefer to be self-sufficient and to be thought a worthy man, than to be involved in many affairs and find my enemies saying: 'he's seaborne cargo, he came where he came from.'" Here the proverbial quotation and the metaphorical reference to life as a sea and man as a seafarer are typical of the Hellenistic moralizing tradition that influenced Roman satire.

Comedy, diatribe, and iambic poetry were the principal Greek literary influences upon Roman satire. Other Greek influences can be traced, most notably in philosophical prose: for example, Lucilius refers to Socratici charti ("Socratic texts": fr. 789 W), which could refer either to Plato's dialogues or to the Socratic writings of Xenophon, and he paraphrases Plato's Socratic dialogue, Charmides (10). Persius's fourth satire also opens with a scene in which Socrates lectures Alcibiades, the material being based on the pseudo-Platonic dialogue Alcibiades I, and Horace, especially in the second book of Satires, was influenced by Socratic writing. But it was the other three Greek genres that gave to Roman satire the source of many of its distinctive features, which were: the castigation of vice and exhortation to virtue; the use of wit and irony; personal attacks and obscenity; the use of metaphor and analogy, often leading to the merging of abstract idea and concrete example (for example, moral vice and physical disease, as in Bion and in Persius's third satire); the loosely structured diatribe with its discursive method and informal transitions; finally, the use of dialogue or of an imaginary interlocutor.

Lucilian Satire

Most of the Greek features that we have identified are to be found in Lucilius (11). His earliest work was in the iambic tradition (books 26-29), but it was his adoption of the dactylic hexameter as the exclusive medium for his satire (books 30 and 1-21) that was his most important contribution to the genre, for this marked a final break with the tradition of the Ennian miscellany. In his "program" in book 26 he describes the audience at which he is aiming [fr. 632-35 W]), not the highbrow intellectuals nor the uncultured masses, but the worthy and moderately cultured men, one of whom Cicero (in a comment on this fragment) calls "a good man and not unlettered." In a word, says Lucilius, "I want to be read neither by the very learned nor by the uneducated." This appeal to a select and moderate audience became part of the traditional program, and in the case of Horace and Persius it had some bearing on their attitude to the problem of freedom of speech, one of the most acute dilemmas of the satirist writing in a society no longer free. Lucilius, indeed, was a man of wealth and social standing, among whose friends were some of his most powerful contemporaries. He was therefore able to speak with frankness, both about himself--which is the privilege of the socially self-

assured--and about his enemies, whom he attacked with a
directness worthy of Archilochus. He himself described
his method: "then let me fly at him with teeth bared
and (blazing) eyes like a dog," a metaphor later adopted by both Horace and Persius (12).

Our brief survey has shown how Lucilius adapted
Greek satiric techniques to Latin hexameter satire. In
the immense range of his subject matter he included
literary and grammatical criticism, and in so doing
introduced to the Roman tradition a fundamental feature. Greek Old Comedy had been a vehicle for literary
criticism, and its most famous example, the debate
between Euripides and Aeschylus in Aristophanes' Frogs,
significantly links the poet's work to moral and social
considerations, that is, to his value as the teacher of
his fellow citizens. We shall see that the connection
between poetry and morality was of primary importance
in Persius. Among Lucilius's fragments is one critical
of the tragedian Accius, and another defending his
criticisms of Homer (13). While literary criticism was
in general important to the satiric tradition, it was
especially significant when it extended to the style,
content, and purpose of satire, so that it was fundamental to the poet's conception of satire. This is
made abundantly clear in the three "literary" satires
of Horace [1.4, 1.10, 2.1] and in the first and fifth
satires of Persius.

Horatian Satire

Horace was much concerned with the definition of
satire, and he shared the ancient respect for the rules
of a particular genre. In the opening lines of Satires
2.1 he sets the scene in terms of a law court, with
himself up on a charge of having broken the laws of the
genre of satire: "there are those who charge me with
being too bitter in my satire and with stretching my
work beyond the law." Like Lucilius (in book 26),
Horace begins his satires with a statement of his
purpose and methods (14). In his first satire Horace
announces that he will castigate vice (in particular
the vice of avarice) and in its place he will put the
virtue of moderation (the Greek sophrosyne): "there is
restraint in things; in a word, there are fixed limits,
either side of which what is right cannot be" [Satire

1.105-6]. As for his style, he will adopt the wit and
irony that marked the Hellenistic diatribe. In Greek
this was called to spoudogeloion (literally "serious
laughing") which Horace neatly turns into Latin with
the words ridentem dicere verum ("to tell the truth
with a smile," line 24). His moralizing, he says, will
indeed deal with serious subjects, but in a lighthearted
style--features of which might be wit, fable, analogy, metaphor, indeed anything that would sweeten the
pill of ethical doctrine. In lines 23-27 he distinguishes between seriousness of purpose and subject on
the one hand, and lightness of style on the other.

In three satires Horace acknowledges his debt to
Lucilius while also criticizing him, and the three give
a good idea of the tradition that Horace inherited and
the changes that he made. After acknowledging his and
Lucilius's debt to Greek Old Comedy in Satires 1.4.1-7,
he goes on to criticize Lucilius for diffuseness and
carelessness in composition [lines 9-13]. Horace himself, he claims, will be more professional in his
writing, above all, more self-critical. He then
defines his own satire, which he ironically refuses to
count as poetry, saying that like that of Lucilius it
shares with real poetry only the characteristic of
meter, in all else being sermo merus ("just prose talk,"
lines 47-48). He quotes from Ennius's epic [lines 60-
61] to establish the difference between his sermones
("talks," that is, satires) and the lofty poetic genre
of epic. Yet Horace gives the lie to his self-irony by
his mastery of poetic technique in this very satire:
the neatly turned phrase (for example, disiecti
membra poetae, ["limbs of the dismembered poet," line
62], in reference to quoting tags from Ennius), and the
vivid metaphor (for example the ink of the cuttlefish
at line 100 for a gossip destroying a friend's reputation, or the life belt of the novice swimmer at line
120 for the young boy helped by the precepts of his
father). Having established his style, Horace can then
return to consideration of his purpose, that is, his
duty as moral critic, which he has outlined with reference to Old Comedy in lines 1-5. This he introduces
with a defense against the charge that he enjoys
hurting the objects of his criticism [line 78], which
Lucilius had also had to answer (15). He further
acknowledges his debt to Lucilius in this section by
adapting Lucilius's appeal to a limited audience [lines

71-78]: "let no bookstall or poster-display have my slim volumes for the sweaty hands of the common crowd to paw over. . . . I recite my work only to my friends, and even then under compulsion." Serious criticism of vice is the satirist's duty, provided it is done with wit [line 91] and good-natured moderation [lines 101-3]. Finally, Horace justifies himself by reference to the precepts of his father [lines 105-29] and, the result of this early training, his own upright character [lines 129-43].

Satire 1.4 is discursive and polemical, and it does not have the self-assurance or literary finesse of its successors, Satires 1.10 and 2.1. Horace was thirty when he published his first book of satires in 35 B.C., and the satire reflects the defensiveness of a young man whose literary and social position was not yet fully assured. It is an important statement of Horace's view of the satirical tradition: while he firmly acknowledges his place in the tradition of Lucilius, he shows by his criticisms of Lucilius how he himself is changing it. Although the two later literary satires show more positive characteristics and even more masterly poetic techniques, the fourth satire sets forth the essential principles of Horace's satire. It is important for an understanding of Persius's place in the tradition.

In Satire 1.10 Horace answers those who had taken exception to his criticism of Lucilius. Granting the good qualities of Lucilius, such as wit and the castigation of vice, he argues again for changes in the tradition. Dealing first with wit [lines 7-19] he says that the satirist's laughter must be tempered by brevity and economy of expression; by variety of mood; finally by irony, for "a smile is more effective than bitterness and often cuts through serious matters better" [lines 14-15]--an excellent statement of the peculiar qualities of Horatian satire. Further he argues for better Latinity, whereas Lucilius had used many Greek words without translating them (lines 20-30), and defends his own efforts to renew Lucilian satire by reference to leading contemporary authors in other genres, such as Vergil in pastoral poetry (lines 31-49). He concludes the passage by emphasizing his own inferiority to Lucilius, the founder (inventor, line 48) of the tradition. This said, he returns to his criticism of Lucilius's undisciplined style [lines 50-

74], repeating his call for self-criticism in Satire
1.4. Finally, he returns to the theme of the satirist's audience [lines 74-91]: a select audience
demands the highest standards of writing, and therefore
of self-criticism. Horace names fourteen of his pauci
lectores ("few readers"), and they include the greatest
writers and literary patrons of the day--Maecenas,
Varius, Vergil, Messalla, and Pollio. In this alone
Horace is claiming a high place for satire in Roman
literary circles. Consequently, it demands the most
polished poetical craftsmanship to be worthy of its
discerning audience.

This is Horace's most forthright statement about his
satire. Five years later, in 30 B.C., he published his
second book of satires, in which the first satire deals
predominantly with the lex operis, the laws of Lucilian
satire. His topics are much the same as in Satires 1.4
and 1.10, but his method is more ironic and more lighthearted. He uses dialogue, defending himself against
the critical advice of the lawyer Trebatius, and he
acquits himself at the end with a punning parody on the
eighth of the Twelve Tables (which were the basic
statement of Roman law). Some critics have dismissed
this poem as frivolous, but it should be seen rather as
adhering to a serious critical position which Horace
has already established in the earlier literary
satires. Its lighthearted irony and brilliant wit are
weapons of a poet who knows that his position is unas-
sailable.

For nearly a century after the publication of
Horace's satires no author of any note attempted to
write in the genre. The reason is simple: freedom of
speech was a thing of the past, and the poet who criticized (or was even thought to be criticizing) the great
ran the risk of exile or execution, or at least the
destruction of his work. Persius therefore inherited
the tradition as Horace had left it.

Conclusion

Horace as a satirist was one of the four "great
shades" whom Dante counted as the greatest of classical
poets, lesser only than Vergil (16). Whether one
agrees with Dante's judgment or not, there can be no
doubt of Horace's originality within the Lucilian tra-

dition. Lucilius had created the hexameter satire
using his own genius on the informal satiric material
inherited from Ennius and the Greek writers. This he
adapted to the Latin language, in itself no mean
achievement. Eventually he disciplined the genre by
the exclusive use of the dactylic hexameter. He
followed the Greeks in his uninhibited attacks on named
contemporaries, so much so that bitterness (acerbitas)
was later considered to be his outstanding characteristic. His immense range and facility led him to write
much that was diffuse and of uneven quality. If we are
to believe Horace, he is rightly to be called the
founder of the genre. His successors all acknowledged
his primacy, but each worked within the Lucilian tradition to alter it. Horace's greatest contribution was
in the tone of his satires, above all in the use of
irony and wit: the phrase ridentem dicere verum ("to
tell the truth with a smile") summarizes the essential
quality of Horatian satire. But there were other
equally significant changes: Horace was a polished
craftsman, even in his earliest work (which includes
the satires), and his mastery of the telling phrase or
the vivid metaphor set a new standard for his successors. Equally sure was his control of language and
meter, and his ironic description of satire as sermo
merus ("mere talk") conceals his range and flexibility
of style and meter, in keeping with a conversational
genre whose material covers a wide range of subject
matter. Horace's versatility allowed him to perfect a
style adequate to the variety of satire. Finally,
Horace brought to satire a new conception of the satirist's "mask" or persona, through which he addressed his
audience. While we cannot judge Lucilius fairly from a
mere collection of fragments, his acerbitas ("bitterness") seems to have been fairly constant, and Horace
says that he was direct in his self-revelation. Horace
is more varied: for example, the satirist who casti-
gates vice in Satire 2.5 is very different from the
persona in the mellow quasi-autobiography of Satires
1.6 and 2.6. The subtle and shifting persona is partly
the result of Horatian irony and poetic flexibility,
and so peculiar to Horace. But he showed the way for
his successors (both in Latin and in later French and
English literature) to use the satirist's persona as an
effective part of satiric technique.
    This then was the satiric tradition inherited by

Persius. His early death and limited output prevented
him from matching the achievements of Horace or of his
successor Juvenal. Like Horace he acknowledged his
debt to his predecessors but established his own originality within the tradition, as an examination of his
satires will show.

Chapter Three

The Prologue and the First Satire

The Prologue

A prologue of fourteen choliambic lines precedes Persius's first or program-satire (1). We have seen that the iambic tradition was important in the transmission of the Greek satiric spirit, and Horace's earliest poems (the Epodes) were written in iambics, sometimes combined with dactylic lines, in the spirit of Archilochus. Although Persius is unique among the hexameter-satirists in using choliambics, Lucilius, like Horace, had written iambics before his satirical hexameters. Persius's older contemporary, Petronius, combined choliambics and dactylic hexameters in one of the verse interludes in his Satyricon [chapter 5]. The meter was also used by nonsatirical writers, for example, by Catullus--more than a century before Persius--whose eighth poem is a moving expression of bitterness and despair after breaking with Lesbia. Quite different in tone are the choliambics of Martial (ca. 90 A.D.) whose epigrams are more in the Greek iambic tradition.

The unusual meter has led some scholars to conclude that the choliambics are not connected with the satires, or even that they are not by Persius. Others believe that these fourteen lines are really two separate seven-line poems. Others again believe that they are an epilogue, rather than the prologue to the satires, since they are placed last in two of the principal manuscripts, while the most important originally omitted them. These problems should not detain us. We may assume, with the majority of scholars, that the choliambics are a prologue to the satires, and we shall see that they are a unity in themselves and linked in tone and theme to the first satire.

The satirist in announcing himself must state his place in the tradition of the genre, reject other genres of poetry (especially epic), and distinguish his chosen genre, satire, from the grander styles of epic and tragedy. All these things Persius does in the first satire, but they are foreshadowed in the prologue, whose general tone claims a lower place for

satire than epic or other poetry that is lofty or
pretentious. Thus Persius adapts Horace's theme of
sermo merus (ironically defining satire as versified
prose) and introduces his own persona with Horatian
irony.

The poem is in two equal parts [lines 1-7, 8-14],
linked by the motif of Pegasus, which appears in the
first and last lines, so as to establish a kind of
ring-composition. The first half deals with Persius
himself as a writer of satire, the second with poets in
general, and the underlying themes are in the first
half, poetic inspiration, and, in the second, poetic
motivation. These are brought together in line 10,
where _ars_ and _ingenium_ (respectively "technical mastery" and "raw genius") are ironically combined. These
terms were basic in the debates about poetry that began
in Alexandria early in the third century B.C. and still
continued in Persius's day. A fundamental problem for
literary critics (including satirists) was to decide
the relative merits of inspiration and technique. Persius here discusses it with the ironic statement that
it makes little difference, because all that matters to
poets and versifiers is being able to earn a meal by
their writing. In fact, he returns to the subject at
great length in the first satire.

He begins his prologue [lines 1-3] with a rejection
of the inspiration claimed in famous passages by Ennius
and Hesiod (2). Ennius had related in his epic how he
had dreamed that Homer had appeared to him on Mount
Parnassus and explained that his soul had transmigrated into the body of Ennius. Ennius, therefore, the
founder of Roman hexameter epic, was claiming to be a
second Homer, sharing the same sources of inspiration
as Greek poets. The Muses, the Greek goddesses of
poetry, were said to inhabit Hippocrene, the fountain
on Mount Helicon that a blow from the hoof of the
winged horse Pegasus caused to gush forth, while Mount
Parnassus was sacred to Apollo, the Greek god and
patron of poetry. Further, among traditional metaphors
for poetic inspiration were drinking from the fountain
of the Muses and dreaming. Persius, therefore, in
these three lines used the traditional symbols for
poetic inspiration to disassociate himself from the
lofty genre of epic, while acknowledging the primacy of
Ennius in that field. By rejecting divine inspiration
Persius placed his satire on a lower lever than other

forms of poetry, and he emphasized the earth-bound nature of satire by using the deflationary vocabulary in the first line, "nec fonte labra prolui caballino" ("I have not wet my lips in the nag's fountain") (3). In the third line ("ut repente sic poeta prodirem" ["that in this way I should suddenly come on stage as a poet"]) he implies that his satire, by contrast, is the result of hard work, not of sudden inspiration, a theme that Horace had on several occasions sounded and one to which Persius returned in the first and fifth satires. In lines 4-7 of the prologue he disassociates himself from pretentious writers, as much as from genuine poets like Ennius. "The Muses and pale Pirene I leave to those whose busts are licked by the clinging ivy"--an adaptation of lines by Horace, who had described a certain bad poet, Fannius, as "happy . . . with his bust" [Satire 1.4.21-22]. Elsewhere, however, Horace claimed the ivy-wreath as the reward of the truly inspired lyric poet [Carmina 1.1.29-32], yet this does not make Persius inconsistent, since he claims to be as far from inspired as from bad poets, and lyric poetry was held to be more lofty than satire. Persius ends the first half of the prologue with a positive statement of what he is after the negative terms of the first five and a half lines: "ipse semipaganus/ad sacra vatum carmen adfero nostrum" ("I, half-initiated, offer my poetry as the poets' rites"). He uses the traditional term vates ("bard") for poets, and adapts the common metaphor of the poets' calling as a sacred ritual so as to deflate his own satire. He is "half-initiated" because, while he does not write sermo merus ("mere prose"), he cannot fully participate in the poets' mysteries as he does not share the divine inspiration of the epic and lyric writers. As semipaganus ("half-initiated") he draws his inspiration from the everyday world of the common man (at least, this seems to be one inference to be drawn from the word), a claim that he repeats in the fifth satire, line 14; verba togae sequeris ("you follow the words of the ordinarily dressed citizen").

In these seven lines Persius states his relationship to other genres of poetic writing (good and bad) and gives the character of his own satire, which is in the middle position, below the lofty inspiration of the Muses but above the specious productions of self-anointed bards. The brevity of these few lines is deceptive, for they are a comprehensive announcement of the satirist's position.

In the second half [lines 8-14] Persius develops the theme of poetic motivation, building his statement around bird-imagery--parrots, crows, and magpies. The parrot and the magpie are well-known imitators. Petronius, for example, has a magpie in a golden cage greet Trimalchio's guests, and the crow, besides being an imitator, is a symbol of foolish pretension, the character in which it appears in one of Aesop's fables. The crow also appeared in Hellenistic choliambics. A third-century A.D. writer, Athenaeus, preserves for us two Hellenistic children's songs in which children greet the coming of spring by visiting houses in the disguise of birds and asking for small presents, much as in the American autumn custom of "trick or treat" (4). In the first song the beggars are disguised as crows and their song is called a "crow-song" or Koronisma. Its author was Phoenix of Colophon, and its meter is choliambic. It is possible that Persius had the song in mind as he introduced the corvos poetas ("crow-poets") into his own choliambics. If so, the begging motif of Phoenix's poem is appropriately transferred to the versifiers of Persius's prologue.

Persius asks the question, "Who trained the parrot [to squawk] 'Hullo!' and taught the magpie to try our (nostra) words?" and answers with "The stomach, master of techniques (ars) and giver of inspiration (ingenium), skilled teacher of words that are denied (by nature)" [lines 8-11]. There is irony here, for we have already seen how Persius is touching on the literary debate between ars and ingenium. The word nostra in line 9 is also significant following so closely on its use (carmen . . . nostrum) in line 7. Persius's implication is that he [line 7], a half-initiate, is at least a genuine satirist without pretentiousness. The hungry parrots and magpies, by contrast, are claiming skills and inspiration that they neither understand nor possess. Nor is hunger their only motive, for greed [line 12] also "inspires" them, with its glittering and deceptive hopes. With such motives poets and poetesses, who are no more than uninspired and unnatural imitators, write poems in a lofty style and lay claim to the Muses' inspiration: "you would believe crow-poets and magpie-poetesses are chanting the nectar of Pegasus" (lines, 13-14, that is, are writing poetry

that is divinely inspired by the Muses). Since in
lines 1-3 Persius has established his distance from
Hippocrene, Parnassus, the Muses, and the poetry they
inspire, his position remains consistent to the end of
the poem.

The choliambic meter, with its Hellenistic and
earlier Greek associations combined with Persius's
adaptation of Horatian irony, makes this poem a striking introduction. In style it foreshadows Persius's
satiric techniques: most conspicuous are brevity of
expression and literary allusion (for example, to
Ennius in lines 1-3, to Horace in lines 5-6, to Callimachus in line 8, to Phoenix in line 13, to Pindar in
line 14). There is effective use of rhetorical
figures, for example in the alliteration of lines 3-4
and 13-14, where the harsh guttural c and the explosive
p reinforce the author's scorn. Most important, however, is the skilled way in which Persius assumes his
persona. As a satirist he comes forward as successor
to Horace and Lucilius, removed from the tradition of
Greek-inspired epic, and a genuinely original artist,
whose own form of inspiration (which he expands upon in
the first and fifth satires) is divided by a wide gulf
from the specious productions of imitative scribblers.
He links himself to the iambic tradition of the Hellenistic writers, and at the same time sets forth his
satirical, Lucilian character. His Muse is the Musa
pedestris ("prosaic Muse") of satire and iambic, earth-
bound, as opposed to the divinely inspired Muse of
epic. Having thus introduced himself, he is ready to
embark upon his program-satire.

The First Satire

The poem is in the form of a dialogue, although the
interlocutor does not have a clearly defined character
like those of Trebatius and Teiresias in the first and
fifth satires of Horace's second book, as Persius himself admits at line 44: "whoever you are whom I have
just introduced as an adversary." Its purpose is to
set forth Persius's program, that is, to give his
apologia for the writing of satire and to distinguish
his poetry from the inferior literary activity of his
contemporaries. The corruption of contemporary literature is shown to be inextricably linked to moral cor-

ruption, so that the wider theme of the moral weakness
of Rome underlies the satirist's literary apologia.

In structure the satire is Horatian, for an apparently informal series of transitions, in the tradition
of satirical sermo, conceals a controlled organization.
The outline of the structure is as follows: 1-12:
introduction--the satirist justifies his writing of
satire because contemporary standards of judgment are
worthless; 13-43: description of contemporary literary
activity, with its authors' pretentiousness and lust
for applause; 44-62: the satirist will earn such
applause as he can because his standards are true and
his self-criticism rigorous; 63-106: examples of
modern literary style are quoted and ridiculed as
frivolous products of literary dabblers and not the
result of a true poet's or orator's labors; 107-34:
epilogue: in reply to the interlocutor's warning, the
satirist justifies his frank criticism by appeal to the
examples of Lucilius and Horace. His discovery of the
rottenness of contemporary standards is a secret, to be
shared only with those few who appreciate the honest
criticism of the satirical tradition.

Persius further establishes the unity of the poem by
linking its introduction and epilogue. The theme of
the satirist's select audience, introduced in lines 1-
3, is resumed in lines 123-26. Second, the question
left incomplete at line 8 ("nam Romae quis non" ["for
who at Rome does not"]) is finished at line 121:
"auriculas asini quis non habet?" ("Who does not have
donkey's ears?"). Thus the ring is closed, and the
primary theme of the corruption of contemporary standards unites the beginning and end of the poem.

The poem begins with homage to Lucilius and Horace.
The first line is a direct quotation from Lucilius,
while the setting of the dialogue between satirist and
interlocutor is like the opening of Horace's second
book of Satires. Moreover, the motif of the select
audience is, as we have seen, part of the satirical
program established by Lucilius and Horace. So Persius
immediately puts himself in the tradition, while forth-
rightly announcing his subject. With his first words,
"O curas hominum! O quantumst in rebus inane!" ("O,
the worries of mankind! How empty is their activity!"),
the satirist in the first line sets himself apart from
the society that he will criticize, whose vanity (in
every sense of the word) will be shown up in contrast

to the integrity of the Stoic poet. "No one will read you," objects the interlocutor, but Persius replies that so corrupt are the standards of Rome that he must write without thinking of popularity. At this point [line 8] he begins the question--"nam Romae quis non . . .?" ("for who at Rome [does] not . . .?")--that will be completed in line 121, and so leads into the main body of the satire. For the moment he breaks the question off, and in a series of jerky, conversational phrases leads up to his self-description as a sardonic observer of human hypocrisy (5). Roman society is referred to in epic terms ("Polydamas and the Trojan ladies," line 4); it prefers bad poets to true ones [4-5]; its scales of judgment are out of balance [5-7]; everyone has ------[8] (what they have comes at line 121). In the meantime the satirist sees the specious severity of adult Roman citizens. Knowing how false the facade is, all he can do is laugh [9-12].

The introduction is an excellent example of Persius's method. He uses traditional motifs, yet establishes his originality, and he sets himself apart from the moral and literary standards of Rome, sure of his own right judgment, unaffected by popularity. Finally, his persona is established as one who reveals others' hypocrisy and expresses his indignation with a laugh.

At line 4 Persius refers to the Romans as <u>Troiades</u>, with more than a hint that the phrase "Trojan women" includes Roman men, a forewarning of the particular approach that he will take in describing the rottenness of society. In lines 13-43 he unites the themes of literary and moral corruption as he describes contemporary literary activity. Beginning with the process of composition [13-14], he describes the recitation of the finished product [15-23] and its effect on author and audience. Writers shut themselves up, their purpose being to produce some piece of pretentious bombast (Persius's scorn is emphasized by the very rare word <u>praelargus</u> ["ultra-enormous"] and by allusion to a passage in Horace [<u>Satire</u> 1.4.19-21] where the underlying metaphor of the bellows is made explicit). As he describes the author's recitation the metaphor changes from the hot air of the bellows to sexual perversion, and lines 15-23 combine with astonishing compression vivid description, moral criticism, and sexual imagery. It is a strangely compelling passage that introduces the reader to the simultaneously attractive and repellent qualities that are typical of Persius. His criticism includes author and audience, so that he is attacking all of Roman society, not just individuals. The spotlight is turned upon the author, freshly groomed and dressed in a new toga with his best ring adorning his finger, as he takes his place upon the dais. So far the emphasis has been on affectation, but the preliminaries to the actual reading are couched in sexual terms [17-18]: "You will rinse your supple throat with a clearing tune-up gargle, effeminate yourself, with wantonly roving eye" (6). The effect upon the audience of Roman aristocrats is to be expected. The poems are pictured as a sexual organ, entering and stimulating the inmost parts of the audience [19-21], and again the ambiguous vocabulary combines literary and sexual imagery. The mutual gratification of effeminate poet and depraved audience reaches its climax in 22-23: "do you, you old man, collect titbits for others' ears, to whom you may say--with your gouty joints and swollen skin--'stop, stop!'?" Since the poet is physically incapable of sexual gratification, his poems perform that task for his audience, who, in their turn, stimulate his lust for applause. Thus the act is consummated as poet and audience mutually indulge their desires, the one for praise, the other for sexual stimulation. Literature has become a barren activity whose purpose is the gratification of debased lusts, and it is symptomatic of the moral rottenness of Rome (7).

At this point the interlocutor breaks in: what is the point of the poet's studies, if his poetry cannot burst forth, like yeast rising or a fig-tree's roots cracking a pavement? Persius replies with scorn, asking if lust for applause is the reason for the poet's pallor and haggard look [24-27]. The interlocutor persists [28-30]: it is worth the effort, he says, to become a figure to be pointed at (the ambiguity is intentional) and to be a textbook for schoolboys. To this Persius replies with a second description, this time of a dinner party of effete aristocrats (30-35: Romulidae at 31, like Titos in 20, is an ironically coined epic form, "sons of Romulus"). Over the wine they discuss poetry and one of them, dressed up in a blue cloak, recites some emotional lines from contemporary tragedies, pronouncing the words effeminately, as if he were straining them like a ripe grape that has been gently burst by pressure of the tongue on the palate. Or, continues Persius with a typical juxtaposition of images, the reciter deliberately mispronounces the words in an affected way, as if they were being unbalanced like a wrestler whose opponent trips him up. Lines 32-35, with their involved metaphors of the nose, filtering, and wrestling, resume the motifs introduced in the earlier descriptions of the recitations, namely that poetic activity is an affectation, and its practitioners and its admirers are no more than effeminate frauds. The applause is heroic, Persius goes on, with a mock-epic phrase (36: <u>adsensere viri</u>, "the heroes approved"), and the poet's ashes will rest the happier in their tomb. The other guests applaud [38]--will not violets blossom upon his grave? "You are ridiculing poetry with your mockery," replies the interlocutor, "what poet would not prefer popularity and a place for his works in a library to their becoming wrapping-paper for fish or spices?"

In the short space of thirty-one lines Persius puts the literary scene before his reader. Author and public are exposed, and the interconnection between literary and moral perversion is established by vivid description and compressed imagery. The poet's progress is described from conception of the poem to his posthumous reputation, and the gloomy picture remains consistent. Poet and audience are motivated by false values, for the fame sought by the former and bestowed by the latter is worthless, worth no more (it is implied) than the ignominious neglect of having one's publications used as wrappers for fish.

Yet the interlocutor deserves a reasoned answer to his question [41-43], which Persius supplies in the next section [44-62], as he discusses the true grounds for poetic fame. The key here is in lines 48-50: "I deny that the final test and limit of what is right is 'well done' and 'how nice!'" The satirist, like any human being, welcomes praise for a job well done. He objects to praise for poetry that does not deserve it, like bad epics or after-dinner poems or the verse of elegant dilettantes [49-53]. Such applause is as undeserved and immoral as that for the recitation described in lines 15-23, or else [53-55] it is no more than the insincere flattery of a client in return for a cheap meal or some cast-off clothing. "How can the truth be told in a society whose values are so perverted?"

continues Persius. In fact the noble poetaster is
physically repulsive, like his poetry. Fat and
bloated, he cannot, like the two-headed god Janus, see
the derogatory gestures being made behind his back.
That is where the truth will be found [56-62].

In itself this is a vigorous passage, distinguished
by lively dialogue and the well-chosen phrase (for
example, rara avis, "a rare bird," Persius's self-
deprecating metaphor for his own poetry that may be
deserving of praise), and by the vigorous description
of the mocking animal gestures in lines 58-60--the
fingers imitating the stork's bill, the hands imitating
the donkey's ears, and the tongue stuck out "as long as
that of a thirsty Apulian dog." But it is also a
logical completion of the argument in the earlier sections, and brings the first half of the satire to a
suitable conclusion. The scales of judgment are out of
the true (compare lines 5-7), and authors and public
are caught in a system of mutual self-deception. Literature and the society for which it is written are
perverted and false.

Persius now turns to consider contemporary poetry as
it actually is [63-106] in a series of four exchanges
with the interlocutor. First the interlocutor praises
its smooth technical perfection and its flexibility
[63-68]. To this Persius replies that these qualities
are achieved by writers who are no more than dilettante scribblers in the Greek fashion, for they cannot
deal with the traditional subjects of Roman poetry nor
(it is implied) recognize the old Roman virtues symbolized by the hero Cincinnatus. It is these Greek
effusions that earn the Greek word euge ("well done!")
as applause, which Persius has already dismissed in
line 49.

"If it is archaic virtue you want," replies the
interlocutor, "why, there are contemporary writers who
are devoted to Accius and Pacuvius" (Roman tragic poets
of the second century B.C.), each of whom is appropriately qualified by an adjective expressive of gnarled
antiquity [76-78]. Persius's reply [79-91] is unyield-
ing: archaizing is as much a sign of decadence as
ultramodern smoothness, and it is symptomatic of the
same moral weakness. Small wonder that boys learn such
a hodge-podge of styles in their schools of rhetoric
(Persius's expressive phrase is sartago loquendi, "a
casserole of speech"). It is derivative and meretri-

cious [79-82], stimulating in its audience the same
depraved sensuality as in the recitation of lines 15-
23--"the knight, plucked smooth, fidgets in ecstasy
upon the benches." The "benches" of line 82, which
could refer equally to those of the recital-hall or of
a law-court, lead in lines 83-87 to a law-court scene
that corresponds to the earlier recitation. Modern
education leads to the same depravity in forensic
rhetoric as in poetic activity. An elderly man defends
himself in court, and his speech aims not so much at
his acquittal as at applause: "wishing to hear the
restrained approval of 'How elegant!'" Persius uses
the Latin word decenter here for the Greek euge of
lines 49-75, but the effect is the same: rhetoric,
like poetry is debased and thrives on the perverted
interaction of speaker and audience. This is put yet
more bluntly as he imagines someone defending himself
on a charge of theft and winning applause for his
"shaven antitheses" and "scholarly figures of speech."
The applause here is bellum ("how nice!"), which again
had been dismissed in line 49. If this is bellum,
concludes Persius, then the Romans have sunk to the
depths of perversion [87]: an, Romule, ceves ("[is it
"nice"] or, Romulus, are you shaking your buttocks?").
The coarse word, ceves, with its homosexual associations, expresses the moral depravity that Roman literary activity reveals, and the reference to Romulus (the
heroic founder of Rome) emphasizes how low his descend-
ants have sunk. In the final four lines of the passage
Persius draws the conclusion [88-91] that these con-
trived speeches, like dilettante poetry, are frivolous
and artifical. Something that will truly affect Persius, as a man who has true standards by which to
judge, must be genuine, the result of long and pains-
taking labor: "he who wants to bow me down with his
sad tale will do it with real tears, not ones got up
the night before."

The interlocutor now returns to contemporary poetry,
and, as in lines 63-66, praises it for its smooth
technique and elegant versification [92]. He quotes
[93-95] as examples parts of three lines which are
notable for their Greek vocabulary and imagery: the
absence of elision; a bold metaphor ("we took a rib
from the long Appennines"); and, finally, a spondaic
ending (that is, four long syllables [----] instead of
the regular ending consisting of a dactyl [a long and

two short syllables, -uu] followed by a spondee [--]).
All these qualities are typical of Alexandrianism, that
is, they display the elegant artificiality of the Hellenistic poets of Alexandria and their Latin imitators,
as opposed to the more vigorous style of the Roman
masters of the hexameter, above all Vergil. The interlocutor here quotes the opening words of the Aeneid as
an example of language that is "frothy, with a fat bark
like a huge dried-up old cork-tree" [96-97]. Very
well, replies Persius, what is there that is "soft, to
be recited with a relaxed neck?" [98]--here his choice
of words recalls the perverted recitation of lines 15-
23, especially lines 17-18. The interlocutor falls
into the trap as he recites four lines [98-101] on a
Dionysiac subject, whose subject matter, emotionalism,
vocabulary, and rhythm are worlds removed from the
Roman virility of Vergil (8). In his scornful reply
[103-6] Persius seizes on the sensuality of these affected lines dismissing them as emasculated, like their
author, who is a moral eunuch and "wet" (in every sense
of the word), floating in the saliva on the poet's
lips. Finally, in keeping with their delicate affectation, they are not the result of the true poet's
agonies of composition, for "they do not beat their
fists on the headboard, there is no flavor of nails
bitten to the quick."
    So ends the main part of the satire and Persius's
attack on contemporary literature and morals. At this
point the reader would do well to reread lines 13-106.
The twin themes of literary and moral rottenness are
consistently developed, and Persius establishes his
independence from the prevailing Hellenism of the day,
with the implication that the decline from the standards of the best of Roman literature is symptomatic of
a collapse in Roman morality. The framework of the
recitation [15-23], the law-court [81-87], and the
second recitation [98], allows Persius to interweave
repeated sexual and eating metaphors with which he
colors his picture of the moral and literary depravity
of Neronian Rome.
    In the epilogue [107-34] Persius returns to the
central figure of the introduction, the satirist himself. In lines 107-23 he answers the interlocutor's
warning: "why be so critical and run the risk of
alienating Roman society?" The interlocutor's question raises a standard subject in the satiric tradi-

tion which both Lucilius and Horace had dealt with. Persius casts the question in phrases appropriate to his satire: <u>teneras auriculas</u> ("soft little ears") continues the motif of the ears, first introduced at line 22, while the diminutive and the epithet express the scorn for the effeminacy of Roman society that has run through the main part of the poem. Then in repeating Lucilius's and Horace's use of the metaphor of the dog [109-10] Persius links it to the relationship of client and patron (9), which had formerly been one of the pillars of the Roman social order. Now it has become so debased that the satirist can take his stance independent of it. His reply is ironical [110-14]: "I will praise everything, make no criticism. Like the audiences I have just been ridiculing I will applaud society with the fashionable Greek word, <u>euge</u>. Or," he continues, "I will imagine that the upper reaches of society are off-limits. I will heed your notice forbidding anyone to relieve himself within the sacred precincts" (10). Such complaisance is too much and Persius drops the mask of irony to appeal to the example of his predecessors [114-18]. Lucilius castigated society and Horace with his gentler criticism attacked every vice. Persius therefore claims the right to add to the tradition [119-23] even if his satire is only a secret muttering [119]. He will bury his secret discovery, which is "auriculas asini quis non habet?" ("Everyone has ass's ears," 121). Thus the question left unfinished in line 8 is completed, and its appropriateness has been established by the intervening criticism of Roman society and literary activity. The burial, moreover, cannot remain a secret, for everyone knows what happened to the barber's secret in the story of King Midas (11), and Persius knows that his criticism, like that of Lucilius and Horace, will be published. Like them, he will criticize without fear or favor. He refers with mock modesty to his secret as <u>tam nil</u> ("so much nothing"), yet it is worth more than all the inflated epic being written: "I will not sell it to you for any <u>Iliad</u>."

Finally Persius returns to the question of his audience [123-34], with which he had begun [1-7]. The <u>Iliad</u> of Attius and other contemporary productions may be popular, but the satirist writes for the discerning few, whose "ears are well-steamed" [126] from reading the masters of Greek Old Comedy. For the first time

the word _auris_ ("ear") is not used in its diminutive
form (_auricula_), and the satirist has listeners whose
ears are healthy and able to appreciate his poetry.
The common people are described in 127-34. Their sense
of humor is vulgar and childish, and they lack the
sensitivity to appreciate intellectual effort. The wit
of the satirist has a constructive moral purpose, but
the humor of the crowd is uneducated and pointless.
For these people the public gazette and the Roman
equivalent of a soap opera are at the appropriate
cultural level (12). The satirist, it is implied,
stands apart. If the discerning few will listen, that
is good, but in any case he will not compromise his
independence.

Chapter Four
The Second, Third, and Fourth Satires

The second, third, and fourth satires form a loosely connected group around the general theme of subordinating one's desires to the dictates of Stoic philosophy. The third satire is flanked by two much slighter poems, both of which appear to derive from the pseudo-Platonic dialogues entitled Alcibiades. The theme of training the will is developed from different aspects; in the second satire the context is the individual's relationship to the gods, and therefore it discusses prayer, an expression of that relationship. The third satire is concerned with the education of the will, and philosophy is found to provide the answers both to the moral problems raised in this satire and to the problems of prayer raised in the second. The philosopher appears as doctor in the last part of the third satire, and his examination of the "patient" (that is, the student) and the establishment of a standard of virtue (as opposed to the deceptive basis for most men's morality) appropriately introduce the fourth satire, where the student is depicted as a candidate for public office. Here the contrast between the public facade and the individual's inner integrity is most marked, and the necessity of self-knowledge as a prerequisite to virtue is proved. There does therefore seem to be a connection between the three poems, of which the central one (the third satire) is the longest and deals with the crucial subject of education. If this grouping of satires is plausible, then the fifth satire, in which Persius deals most explicitly with his own education, is seen to be the climax of the book. It relates the general principles of satires 2-4 to Persius's particular experience, with the conclusion that he has through philosophy achieved true freedom. The sixth satire, then, with its more relaxed persona, stands as an epilogue to the whole book.

The Second Satire

The second satire has been criticized for its apparent indirection and consequent lack of unity. While Persius is less compelling here than in the other satires (excepting perhaps the fourth), he is undoubtedly in control of his material, and the poem is a coherent entity. It begins with Persius's older friend, Macrinus, sacrificing to his Genius (that is, guardian spirit) on his birthday, as any pious Roman should do. The imagery of the opening seven lines is of openness and honesty, and the birthday is a _dies faustus_ ("a day of good omen"), favored by the gods and therefore a sign of Macrinus's right relationship to them [lines 1-4]. He does not need to bribe them with extravagant vows, nor to pray secretly for things that he dare not admit to other men [lines 4-7]. His thoughts, and therefore his wishes, are honest, and he can pray openly--"aperto vivere voto" ("to live with open prayer")--unlike the majority of mankind.

Macrinus, according to the scholiast, had been a student under Persius's teacher, Servilius, and he therefore stands for the ideal of education that Persius himself achieved (as he will show in satire 5). In the narrower context of the second satire Macrinus's birthday-sacrifice appropriately introduces the theme of prayer, for he is an example of the man whose wishes are in accordance with the precepts of philosophy. He is therefore in contrast with the great majority of upper-class Romans ("bona pars procerum" ["a good part of the nobles," line 5]), with whose hypocrisy the rest of the satire deals. Macrinus is necessary for the satirist to introduce his theme, but, having served his purpose in the introductory lines, he leaves the stage, and the "you" addressed elsewhere in the poem is the satirist's supposed and unnamed adversary. It should be noted that, as in satire 1, Persius is concerned with the morality of the upper class, and he deliberately chooses the _proceres_ in line 5 because if the "great men" are morally rotten, the whole of Roman society also will be. This general theme is repeated toward the end of the satire by the naming of Aurelius Cotta Messalinus ("magni Messalae lippa propago" ["the blear-eyed son of mighty Messala," line 72]) as an example of degenerate Roman nobility.

After the introductory four lines Persius develops

his main theme beginning [lines 5-16] with the prayers of a typical noble. The central theme is hypocrisy, for noblemen live in the public eye but they cannot pray openly. Most must pray silently, so shameful are their real desires. Openly they pray for things that all would approve, and even a philosopher would encourage a sound mind (mens bona), a good reputation, and good credit (both in financial and other contexts). When Persius makes his prayer at the end of the poem [lines 73-74] he concentrates entirely on the mens bona, which is there further defined as

> conpositum ius fasque animo sanctosque recessus
> mentis et incoctum generoso pectus honesto.

> a blend of human and divine duty in the mind, a heart pure in its inmost recesses, and a breast fused with nobility and honor.

The nobleman who is heard praying for mens bona scores an impressive point with his hearers [line 8], but this is so much show. The reality is sordid greed, of which four examples are given [lines 9-14]: prayers for a rich uncle's death (1); for a lucky find of buried treasure; for a sickly ward's death, leaving the guardian as heir to his property; finally, for his wife's death, or, better still, for the deaths of three wives, if one is lucky enough to have married women who die young and leave ample dowries to revert to the widower. The duplicity of these prayers, public and secret, is enhanced by the outward forms of their accompanying ritual [lines 15-16]. So that the prayer may be pure the nobleman performs a ritual ablution in the flowing waters of the Tiber. The irony of "haec sancte ut poscas" ("so that you may make a pure prayer," line 15) becomes fully apparent at line 73 with the description of inner purity, especially sanctos recessus ("pure inmost parts"), that has been quoted above.

At this point [line 17] the satirist asks a simple question: what does Jupiter, to whom the nobleman is praying, think of all this? In this passage, lines 17-30, a further irony is established. The nobleman, who dares not let his prayer be heard by other people, in fact would not want Jupiter himself to understand him. This is proved by supposing that the most venal of Roman judges, here given the name of Staius, were to

hear the prayer: he would be appalled and cry out
"Good God!" If a Staius reacts in this way, what would
God himself say? Just because Jupiter has not struck
the suppliant dead with lightning (the proverbial punishment of blasphemers), it does not mean that Jupiter
is a fool. The conclusion, then, is that the suppliant
thinks Jupiter is a fool when he supposes that the god
can be bribed with the offal from sacrificial victims.
The theme of bribing the gods is constant in the satire. At the beginning [line 3], Macrinus's prayers
were described as not being "bargaining" ("non tu prece
poscis emaci" ["you do not ask with bargaining prayers"]), and the adjective _emaci_ ("bargaining", "for
the purpose of buying") is picked up by _emeris_ in line
30 (from the verb _emere_, "to buy"), which has for its
object the diminutive _auriculas_ ("little ears"), already familiar to us from its pejorative use in the
first satire. Persius returns to the theme in each
section of the poem (see lines 29, 40, 46-49, 55-63, 69-
70), finally to expose its hypocrisy in 71-75.

In lines 31-40 Persius leaves the noble suppliant and
describes the prayers made for him when he was a baby
by his grandmother or superstitious aunt or doting
nurse. It is a vigorous and vivid passage, as the
silly precautions of the women against the evil eye are
described, and their well-nourished hopes are contrasted
with the scrawny infant [line 35]. But in the event
their prayers are no less greedy than the noble suppliant's: "let him be longed for by kings and queens
as their daughter's husband; let him be the girls'
desire; wherever he treads let roses bloom" [lines
37-38]. Their outward forms of purity (wearing a
white dress, line 40), are no less specious than the
ritual washing of lines 15-16, and no less deserving of
Jupiter's denial.

After this glance at prayers for the suppliant,
Persius turns back to him and his prayers for the last
few examples [lines 41-51]. In each case reality shows
up the hollowness of the prayer. First is the prayer
for health and long life (a prayer not to be disap-
proved even by the Stoic), which is contrasted with the
reality of the suppliant's gluttony, a sure way to an
early death [lines 41-43]. Then comes prayer for an
increase in possessions [lines 44-46], negated by the
opulence of the offerings designed to buy the favor of
the gods. Instead they ruin the suppliant [lines 46-51],

for, still living on hope, he spends his last money on extravagant sacrifices. Thus Persius reaches a climax of absurdity in his development of the theme of bribing the gods.

His is able now to turn from examples to the underlying causes of the rottenness of men's prayers [lines 52-70]. Because men value gold, being liable to the passion of greed, they suppose that the gods have the same values. So they gild their statues and use golden utensils in their ritual in a degenerate contrast with the honest simplicity of the ancient Romans. Yet the effect is nothing, for, while men at least get some use from gold, the gods are quite unaffected. "In a holy place what good does gold do? To be sure, just as much as dolls offered by girls to Venus" [lines 69-70].

It would not do for the satirist to leave us on so negative a note, and so he ends his poem [lines 71-75] with the positive answer to the question of what to bring the gods, introduced by the words "quin damus id superis" ("why don't we give this to the gods . . . ?"). Persius's subtlety in shifting the ground of his argument is easily overlooked, but it is impressive evidence of his mastery of satiric techniques. He has started with a good man (Macrinus) thanking the gods on his birthday. The body of the poem is about people trying to buy something from the gods, because their rotten moral values permeate their religion. Now he returns to prayers that are not seeking to get something in return. A good suppliant need not offer an extravagant sacrifice, and his piety is beyond the grasp of a degenerate noble like Messalinus. For it is the offering, that is, the state of mind of the suppliant, that matters. What is prayed for is not mentioned, for it is irrelevant. Therefore the satirist's prayer is not a prayer in the sense that the prayers of lines 5-51 were. Instead it is a state of mind that is at unity with God, inwardly pure, morally upright, in sum, truly noble.

So in the final lines the satirist returns to the spirit of his introduction: only the good man can approach the gods without fear (for superstition is but a form of fear of the gods), and the only offering pleasing to the gods is a mind truly good. How far removed is this <u>mens bona</u> from the hypocrisy of the noble's first prayer in line 5! Prayer is found to be a right state of mind, not a bargaining for divine favor.

This satire has frequently been criticized for its apparently loose structure and its lack of originality. Neither criticism is fully justified. The unity of the poem is maintained by its theme, by the progression of examples leading to the reflective passage that begins at line 52, and by the connection between the examples of a right approach to the gods with which it begins and ends. The weakest point in its structure is the introduction of the women's prayers at 31-40, yet even this is not too abrupt for the loose composition of a conversational satire.

The theme is not original, and most of the doctrines can be found in earlier writers or in Seneca. Many readers, moreover, have been disappointed when they turn to Persius after reading Juvenal's magnificent tenth satire (and its English adaptation, Johnson's Vanity of Human Wishes). Juvenal's poem is on a far larger scale (about five times the length of Persius's poem) and consequently develops its examples in a more leisurely way. Juvenal is concerned with the results of prayer, and his examples are all negative. Persius deals with the attitude of the suppliant, and he proceeds from theme and example [lines 1-57] to reflection on underlying causes [lines 52-70], leading to the positive conclusion [lines 71-75]. The simple theme of the pious and moral suppliant has many parallels, for example the twenty-third Ode of Horace's third book, especially the final stanza. According to Xenophon (2), Socrates had said that piety was not a matter of bargaining with the gods (emporike techne or "commercial skill"), and the pseudo-Platonic dialogue, Second Alcibiades, has enough similarities with Persius to prove that he was treading a well-worn path; nor are the moral examples of the diatribe against gold in lines 59-67 either fresh or inspiring. Yet the poem does have fresh qualities: compact examples, enlivened by vivid phrases and vignettes; lively use of direct speech; vigorous phraseology and vocabulary (for example, the vulgar word ebulliat [literally "bubble out"] for "die" in line 10); sudden flashes of poetic feeling (like the roses in 38); above all, the moral earnestness of the satirist expressed, for example, in the memorable lines at 61-63--all these things are the creation of Persius from the raw material of familiar moral diatribe. He clothes Stoic doctrine in poetic expression, and the result is more successful than many modern critics have been prepared to concede.

The Third Satire

The third satire is concerned with study. It starts with a lazy student and ends with the suggestion that all men need to be students of Stoic ethics, for, in the words of the Stoic paradox, "only the wise are sane." Persius had ended the second satire with the idea of the <u>mens bona</u> ("good mind") as the only acceptable basis for prayer. In this satire he suggests both the need and the way for study leading to the achievement of a "good mind."

The poem falls into two roughly equal parts [1-62 and 63-118]. In the first the focus is upon the student, a young man of ample means and weak motivation. The satirist proves that unless he chooses to study philosophy the young man will have an aimless life, far below his potential as an adult of substantial social position. In the second part the lesson of the first part--that philosophy can give life a purpose--is given a more general application, in which the medical metaphor dominates. The conclusion of the poem rests on the Stoic paradox that only the wise are sane.

The first section [lines 1-34] consists of a scene in which a friend comes upon a young man still snoring in bed, although [lines 5-6] the sun is already high in the heavens (3). The young man knows he ought to be studying; he knows that philosophy will point him to a good life; he knows that his social and financial position [lines 24-29] demands a greater responsibility from him than from people with less at stake in life. Yet sloth is easier. He knows what is better and pursues what is worse. In a sense, then, as Nisbet has said, these lines are a dialogue "between the satirist's higher and lower selves."

The lazy young man lies in bed in the first four lines admitting in the opening words of his soliloquy that "this is the same old story," and so establishing immediately an important point, the insidiousness of sloth. The intervention of the friend stirs him to action [lines 7-14]. Up he gets and immediately is angry because no servants come at his call, and his irritation is increased as he goes to his desk to start writing: his pen is no good, the ink is too thick and then is overdiluted—in short, nothing works. These three scenes [lines 1-14] are brilliantly written. They move speedily from inertia to pointless action, they establish the liability of the student to sloth and anger, and they look toward the aimlessness of life that is explicitly described in the conclusion of the first half of the poem [lines 60-62]. At the same time, the description is so vivid that the reader can immediately identify with the characters, especially if he has had the experience of trying to start writing on a sunny day, when the easiest thing to do is to make excuses for not writing.

The student is making a fool of himself, and is like a young bird or a willful baby bawling for baby-food and refusing to be consoled by his nurse's lullaby [lines 16-18]. At this point the higher self (or friend) lectures him for the rest of the scene [lines 19-34], and it is this persona who speaks for the rest of the satire. He likens the student to a leaky jar, or to clay still to be formed by the potter. His wealth and breeding cannot conceal his immaturity. Nor can he get off so easily as the dissolute and wealthy Natta (a name taken from Horace, who uses it as an example of meanness), for Natta is beyond the reach of philosophy, encased in the fat envelope of vice and sunk beneath its surface. The young student still has the chance to learn what virtue is.

This appropriately introduces a new section in which the persona imagines the worst punishment for the worst sinner, that is a tyrant (who usually metes out punishment to others), lines 35-43. This is to recognize virtue when it is too late to become virtuous: "virtutem videant intabescantque relicta" ("may they see virtue and pine away now that they have left her disregarded" line 38). This, the satirist continues, is a punishment worse than those inflicted in the most famous legendary punishments. This section should be taken closely with the preceding lines: Natta cannot perceive his predicament (stupet vitio ["he is unconscious from vice," line 32]), but the tyrant can, too late. The student, who still has the choice of knowledge (which leads to virtue) or ignorance, has time to grasp the way of virtue.

The idea of choice becomes the leading motif in the

next section [lines 44-62], which closes the first half of the satire and is directly connected with the opening lines, especially in lines 58-59. The satirist recalls his childhood, when he used to pretend that he had an inflammation of the eyes to avoid having to learn Cato's dying speech for recitation to an admiring audience of adults. Understandably, he adds, because his highest goals (summum, a technical term in philosophy for the ultimate good thing to be achieved) was to win at dice or other games that were appropriate activities for a mere schoolboy. By contrast the slothful young man knows the Stoic doctrines and the Pythagorean dilemma, that is, the letter Y, by which Pythagoras had symbolized the choice between virtue and vice (4). The implication is that although he knows the right doctrines he is like the schoolboy who avoided learning Cato's dying words. By referring to the episodes from childhood Persius is reminding his reader of the image of the student as a baby [lines 17-18], and the recall of the opening lines of the poem is completed in the satirist's next words [lines 58-59]--"are you still snoring?" Finally, he summarizes the lazy student's situation: "Do you have a goal, a target at which to aim? Or are you aimlessly throwing broken crocks and mud at crows wherever you find them, not caring where your legs take you and living from day to day?"

The first half of the poem is now complete. The satirist has established that the young man will remain an immature child if he refuses to learn the doctrines of philosophy. But he still has freedom of choice between an aimless existence or the way of virtue. And he still has time to make his choice, for it is not yet too late. Through the succession of vivid scenes and shifting imagery the message is clear.

From this point the poem develops along more general lines. The dominating motif of the second half is the metaphor of disease. The aimless existence of those who have ignored philosophy is like a disease, against which philosophy provides the only defense. Persius emphasizes the prophylactic nature of philosophy, especially in lines 63-64, thus developing the idea, prominent in the second satire, of virtue being a general state of mind rather than a response to a series of particular circumstances. The medical metaphor begins the second half [lines 63-65] and is extended through the parable of the sick man [lines 88-106] and the apparently healthy man [lines 107-18].

First the satirist announces that a cure is too late once the disease has reached its zenith, and that it is better to avoid the doctor's bills by guarding against the onset [lines 63-65]. Then he applies this to the human condition [lines 66-72] by enumerating the basic questions to which philosophy can provide the answer. By studying in good time these problems of psychology, religion, and ethics, one can guard against vice and lack of purpose, things that are analogous to disease. Nor, he continues, should a man grudge the time spent in study even if he has been successful in his career (the lawyer's profession is here chosen as the example, lines 73-76), a repetition of the caution given in lines 24-29, that it is not outward wealth and social position that matter but the character within.

Having given his philosophical lecture without metaphorical language, the satirist meets with a series of reactions. First [lines 77-88] comes the "plain man in the street," whom Persius presents as a rough centurion, elsewhere used by him as an example of vulgar ignorance (Satire 5.189-91). In ten lively lines Persius vividly puts him before us: "What I know is all I need to know. I don't want to be like Arcesilas or Solon weighed down with care, with stooping head and eyes fixed on the ground, mumbling to themselves and gnawing their lips in silence like madmen; they purse their lips as they weigh words in the balance. . . ." Of course this is Persius, not any plain man, who speaks, but it gives a wonderfully direct picture of the philosopher as others see him. The philosophic names are all jumbled up and later the great Epicurean poet Lucretius is parodied [line 84]. Finally, the centurion's audience of "muscular young men" cackle as they join in ridiculing the eggheads [lines 86-87]. Persius in this scene puts a gulf between the ignorant masses and the philosopher, thus making the paradox at the end of the poem ("only the wise man is sane") even more striking. A further part of his satiric irony is that the student, who (it will be recalled) is rich and of the upper classes, is also distanced from the people and therefore already has much in common with the philosopher (5).

Next the satirist illustrates his theme with a story [lines 88-106]: such parables were an important feature of the Roman satiric tradition and earlier of Greek moralizing. In keeping with the medical metaphor he describes a sick man who goes to the doctor and acts on his advice until he starts to feel better. Then he goes back to his old habits of self-indulgence, refuses a friend's advice, and dies. The story ends with the man's funeral as his slaves (now citizens, having been freed by his will) carry him out for burial.

Instead of drawing a moral directly from his parable, Persius turns immediately to another scene that interprets his medical allegory in psychological terms. His hearer responds to the parable by saying "well, there's nothing wrong with me" [lines 107-9], words that recall the opening of the parable, in which the sick man consults his doctor, knowing that there is something wrong with him. The satirist replies that the mind is no less diseased than the body so long as it is subject to the passions of greed, lust, gluttony, fear, and anger [lines 109-18]. The ordinary man, untutored in philosophy, is in fact more mad than Orestes, the outstanding mythological example of madness. And so the poem ends with the Stoic paradox that only the philosopher is sane, so that the lazy student, with whom it began, must study philosophy if he wishes to avoid the madness that afflicts the great majority of mankind.

The third satire is a masterpiece, and its central position in the book is some indication of the weight that Persius attached to it. It is remarkable for its economy, as can be seen from the difficulty of summarizing an already concise poem. It displays the full range of Persius's style to its best advantage. The compact and shifting imagery is used with assurance and consequently with less obscurity; for example, at lines 81-82, the philosophers' mumbling and facial contortions are vividly expressed even though the closely packed metaphors do not allow of an easy and literal translation. The guiding motifs of sloth and disease are used with consistency, and the poem is enlivened by vigorous dialogue and brilliant description. It is the work of an assured artist.

The Fourth Satire

The third satire ends with a person who does not know himself and thinks he is healthy, but is in fact

morally diseased. It is this predicament that is the
principal concern of the fourth satire. The highest
calling of a citizen in a free society is to serve his
fellow citizens in political office, but to do this a
candidate for office must be morally sound, a condition
that can be achieved only after deep introspection.
This is summed up in the Greek proverb gnothi seauton
("Know yourself") which Persius combines with the Stoic
paradox "Only the wise man is beautiful," to expose the
hypocrisy of candidates for public office. The dramatic setting at the beginning of the satire is fifth-
century Athens, with the talented and unprincipled
Alcibiades standing for office and being dissuaded by
Socrates, because his moral principles are not solid
enough. The Greek setting is appropriate, because the
democracy of Athens was a context in which, in principle at least, the best person could be elected by the
people. This was not the case in Rome of Persius's
time, ruled by a young autocrat and without free elec-
tions. Yet the question of public service was still
extremely important, especially to the Stoics. The
Stoic Seneca, for example, served as Nero's principal
adviser for the first eight years of his reign. Persius's friend Thrasea Paetus, the most outspoken of
Nero's opponents and another leading Stoic, served as
consul and senator, only withdrawing from political
activity in 62 when differences with Nero made his
position untenable. Political service was still very
much a possibility for Stoics under Nero, especially
before 62, when Seneca retired from court and Nero
became more autocratic. Sixty-two was also the year of
Persius's death, so that when he was writing there
still was significant political activity among Stoics.
It is certainly not necessary, and probably wrong, to
see any reference to Nero in Persius's Alcibiades (6).
Persius uses Alcibiades because he was a familiar example of a political paradox, at once capable of brilliant leadership and squalid ethics. In a rhetorical
handbook published some thirty years before Persius
wrote, the author, Valerius Maximus, cannot decide
"whether Alcibiades' good points or vices were more
destructive to his state, for with the former he
deceived his fellow citizens, and with the latter he
damaged them" (7).
     Alcibiades was also familiar as an example in the

philosophical literary tradition. Persius must have used the pseudo-Platonic dialogue, First Alcibiades, for his general setting and some particular expressions (8). For example the opening words of the satire ("rem populi tractas?" ["Are you entering politics?"]) imitate Socrates' words "Are you intending soon to offer yourself as a political guide for the Athenians?" [Alc. I. 106c]. Another Socratic dialogue that contributed to the fourth satire is Plato's Symposium, where [216a] Alcibiades says: "He is forcing me to admit that I am very inadequate, not giving attention to my own character while taking a leading part in Athenian politics." Persius therefore transfers a well-known philosophical example from Socrates' Athens to Neronian Rome. As in the two preceding satires, he moves from an individual in a particular situation to a general discussion. In the fourth satire the technique is less satisfactory because of the confusion between Athens and Rome, but this does not affect the vigor of the satire or its didactic content.

The poem falls into three parts. In the first [lines 1-22] Socrates, as the satirist's persona, shows Alcibiades that his moral development is inadequate to justify putting himself forward as a political leader. He is intellectually precocious and knows the difference between right and wrong. But his motives are base: he is hungry for popularity, "wagging his tail like a dog," and his aim in life (summa boni or "highest good") is to live comfortably and tan himself in the sun (a symbol of luxury). Finally, Alcibiades' claim that his high birth justifies his political ambition cannot conceal his poor moral condition. His principles are no different from those of a ragged peasant herb-seller [19-22] who wants to please her public and enjoy its rewards just like Alcibiades.

There is some continuity here with the third satire, in which the student was comfortably off but lazy, and still had the choice of acquiring the knowledge of virtue. In this satire Alcibiades is also young and rich, but he has gone through the motions of studying philosophy. Socrates shows that even this knowledge is deceptive without a genuinely good character. There is therefore a progression from the third satire. In the fourth the student is still found to be inadequate, and the test comes in the most important field of public

activity, that is, politics. Here, just as in one's
private life, thorough self-knowledge is an essential
prerequisite.

The satirist, no longer speaking through the medium
of Socrates, develops the theme of self-knowledge in
the second part of the poem [lines 23-41]. Adapting a
parable of Aesop he imagines men walking through life
each with a knapsack on his back containing his faults
(9). All men watch the next man's knapsack, none his
own: "Ah, no one, no one at all, tries to delve deep
into himself! Every man watches the knapsack on the
back of the man before him." This is then illustrated
by two examples. First, two men are imagined gossiping
about a rich but mean Roman. Next, the criticism turns
on the young Alcibiades himself, who is imagined as a
homosexual luxuriating in the sun (the same image as
had appeared in line 18) and making his body smooth and
attractive to his lover. But someone nearby jogs by
him and tells him the truth in abusive terms. Nothing
can change Alcibiades from what he is.

These nine lines [33-41] are undeniably obscene and
unattractive. But we should remember that since obscenity was an integral part of the satiric tradition
Persius is doing no more than use a well-known technique to illustrate his theme. The intimate physical
details are put in to jog the reader's attention.
This, the satirist is saying, is the sort of thing
other people think about us, and we would do well to
know ourselves in depth before exposing ourselves to
public criticism.

The moral is drawn in the concluding section [lines
45-52]. We criticize others and are ourselves targets
for criticism. Deep down we are diseased (or, as
Persius puts it, "you have a wound hidden deep in your
groin"), but we present a fine facade to the world.
"Well," replies the young man, "if everyone thinks me a
fine person why shouldn't I believe them?" The reply
is inexorable: if you are liable to the passions of
avarice, lust, and greed (10), then you are not a fit
candidate for public office, and your public life will
be a fraud. "Repudiate what you are not: let the
vulgar people take back their gifts. Live by yourself
and learn how barely you are furnished" [lines 51-52].

Despite its obvious shortcomings, this is an interesting and at times vigorous satire. It uses a
well-known Greek example in a Roman context, and its

didactic purpose is both consistent with Persius's other satires and universal in its application. With the equally slight second satire it makes an appropriate foil for the weighty third satire, and the three poems together give a consistent examination of the Stoic doctrine on training the mind and will, preparatory to the fifth satire, which is the climax of Persius's book.

Chapter Five
The Fifth and Sixth Satires

The fifth satire contains the most personal revelations in Persius's poetry. It is by far the longest of the six satires, 191 lines out of a total of 650. In it Persius draws together the different themes of the earlier poems, both the programmatic statements on poetry and morality in the choliambics and the first satire, and the examinations of the training of the mind and will that occupy the second, third, and fourth satires. To bring this wide range of subject matter into a comprehensive compass the satirist adopts two personae. In the first part [lines 1-51] he is the pupil of Cornutus, learning the craft of poetry and a philosophy for life in harmonious friendship with his teacher. He abandons this subordinate persona at line 52 and for the rest of the poem speaks as a graduate rather than a student (there is a last tribute to the teaching of Cornutus in lines 62-65). His second persona is, in technical terms, that of the Stoic *proficiens* and his subject the freedom of the person who has become "proficient" in Stoic philosophy. This freedom [*libertas*, line 73] is discussed and defined, and the basis of the discussion is the famous Stoic paradox "Only the wise man is free" (1). Thus Persius delineates the end result of Stoic discipline. He, as a poet who has the free mastery of his medium and as a human being who is free to make correct moral choices, has achieved freedom through the rigorous discipline of Stoic training.

Many critics have been unhappy with the loose structure of this poem. The changing personae, the succession of scenes, examples, and dialogues, and the close-packed images and metaphors do indeed make it a difficult satire to comprehend on a first reading. Yet a closer examination reveals its unity, both within the poem itself and in its relationship to the preceding satires, while the progression of thought is logical. Persius begins with style and poetry, which lead him to recall his training as a young man. The education of

54

the young poet cannot be separated from his training in ethics and philosophy (see lines 36-40), and this leads away from personal recollection to a consideration of mankind in general. After many examples the contrast between the "wise man" (that is, Persius as the successful student of Cornutus) and the great mass of the rest of humanity is fully drawn. As in the first satire, the poet remains alone and independent, truly free, unlike the rest of mankind. The contrast is epitomized in the closing lines, where the poet-philosopher's words are dismissed as worthless by a vulgar centurion. Here Persius subtly brings the poem full circle. In the last line the figure of one hundred is prominent ("I'd offer a short 100 pennies for 100 Greeks"), and in the first two lines of the satire the word centum ("one hundred") appears no less than three times. This detail makes quite clear that Persius saw the poem as a coherent unit.

The first twenty-nine lines are concerned with the same subject as the choliambics and the first satire, poetry and the appropriate style for the satirist. Persius announces that "bards" (he uses the pretentious word vates for a poet) "like to call for one hundred voices for themselves, one hundred mouths and one hundred tongues with which to declare their poems" (2). The cliché refers to poets of the lofty genres of tragedy and epic [lines 3-4], from which Persius has already dissociated himself in his Prologue and program-satire. As in the first satire, an interlocutor (generally taken to be Cornutus himself) cuts short his flight of epic bombast with a series of lively images reminding him of his more earth-bound poetic calling. Some of these repeat earlier passages. In the choliambics, for example, Persius had described himself as semipaganus ("half-initiated") in bringing his poetry to the "rites of the bards." He dissociated himself there from the standard sources of poetic inspiration, Parnassus and Helicon (homes respectively of Apollo and the Muses), and he referred to the crowd of would-be poets as "crows and magpies." In the present passage the interlocutor advises him to leave Helicon to those who aim at the lofty styles of epic or tragedy [lines 7-9], and in a series of images describing the bombastic poet he uses the phrase "ineptly cawing like a crow" [line 12]. Even without these references, however, the interlocutor's speech here is one of Persius's most forthright expositions of the style and content of his satire. "You [Persius] follow the language of ordinary Romans, skillfully joining words for sharp effect. Your style is well-rounded, free from excess. Expertly you scrape away unhealthy vices and with a free man's wit you nail wrong doing. Let this [that is, ordinary life] be the source of your words" [lines 14-17].

In reply the satirist [lines 19-21] agrees that the bombastic trivialities of tragedy are not for him, and he adds, in a memorable phrase, _secrete loquimur_ ("My words are for a select audience"). Thus in a few lines Persius has set forth the principles of his poetry and defined his audience. His poems are so cleverly composed and their ethical content is so far above the standards of common men, that they can be read only by a select few. Thus he sets his distance from the ambitious efforts of more popular authors. Having thus established his independence as a creative artist, he is in a position to offer objective criticism of contemporary ethics, which will be the subject of the main part of the poem (lines 52 onward).

First, however, he must reveal the source of his poetic craftsmanship and of his knowledge of philosophy (referred to in lines 14-16). It is none other than Cornutus, the philosopher and literary critic who was Persius's friend and preceptor for the last twelve years of his life. In the first part of this personal address [lines 21-29] Persius praises Cornutus as a literary critic. Having established that he is writing for a select audience and having dissociated himself from the Greek genres of tragedy and epic, Persius claims the encouragement of the Muse of Roman poetry to assure Cornutus of his sincerity (3). In a succession of images [22-29] he promises to reveal the inmost secrets of his heart for Cornutus to shake out like the folds of a cloth or to tap on as a test for solidity as one might test a plastered wall. He will drag out from the inmost recesses of his heart secrets that cannot be revealed in words. Yet his words will break the seal. And it is for this, the sincere expression of uncontrived poetic thought, that he could justifiably ask for the traditional one hundred voices.

The whole passage is an important and brilliant statement about the purposes of Roman satire, and it expresses more comprehensively the ideas sketched in the choliambics and the first satire. Persius justifies his standing apart from the more widely read genres of tragedy and epic. As befits the friend and student of the great critic Cornutus, he claims that his poetry is sincere, lacking in the gaudy attractions of contemporary "best-sellers." Sincerity of expression means trying to put into words thoughts that lie too deep for facile expression [line 29], and this, too, justifies the complexities of his satiric style. Thus Persius, starting from a similar position to that of Horace, builds on his great predecessor's work, and justifies his own innovations in the genre of Latin satire (4).

In the next passage [lines 30-51] Persius fulfills the promise of lines 21-29. It is usually assumed that those lines refer only to the expression of Persius's friendship with Cornutus, and that lines 30-51 refer only to the past debt of student to teacher. If this were so, it would be hard to argue for the unity of the whole poem, nor could one reasonably justify the intense language of lines 26-29. Lines 30-51 in fact continue the introduction, leading up to the main body of the poem that begins at line 52. In them Persius indirectly justifies his moral purpose. The two principal subjects of his satires are poetry and ethics: in the first satire he had shown how the two could not be separated, and his attitude is the same in the fifth. In the first part of the introduction [lines 1-29] he had explained and defended his poetic principles, techniques, and purpose; in the second he justifies his credentials as a moral critic by recalling his training under Cornutus. The passage, it is true, is an eloquent testimonial to Cornutus as a friend and teacher, and as a personal statement it is unique in Roman satire (5). But it also expresses how intertwined are the thoughts of the two men: therefore, it follows, when Persius makes moral criticism of Roman society (as he will do in lines 52-188), he speaks with the authority of Cornutus. Lines 30-51, therefore, are the continuation of and foil to lines 1-29 justifying Persius's claim to be a moral critic.

In describing his relationship to Cornutus, Persius uses two guiding metaphors, of which the first is that of father and son. After six lines describing his situation "at the crossroads of life" [line 35], he emphatically says "me tibi supposui" ("I made myself

your child," line 36) and describes how Cornutus, like
a father, acknowledged him: "teneros tu suscipis annos/
Socratico, Cornute, sinu" ("You took my tender years up
in your Socratic embrace"). The Latin words supposui
and suscipis belong to the vocabulary of parenthood,
for the newborn infant was placed (supponere) at the
feet of the father, who signified acceptance of pater-
nal responsibilities by lifting him up (suscipere) in
his arms. Persius's metaphor is striking, since the
end of adolescence to most people is a "commencement"
(as we may call it) of responsibility as an independent
adult. Persius, however, realized that, although he
had reached physical and legal manhood, he was an
infant morally, with Cornutus as his moral "father."
The image of Cornutus as father is filled out in lines
37-40 by metaphors descriptive of him as teacher and
moral guide. He provided the canon (regula or "rule")
by which to "straighten crooked morals," and he
fashioned Persius's mind as an artist fashions a por-
trait-head in wax or clay.

    The second guiding metaphor of the passage [lines
30-51] is that of harmony, a basic concept in the
thought of Plato and many Greek thinkers, including the
Stoics. The word literally refers to things "fitting
together." In philosophy it was used by Plato especially in the psychological and moral context of a soul
whose parts are in harmonious union, and by the Stoics
of the philosopher living in harmony with nature.
These are the principles underlying Persius's description of his life with Cornutus [lines 41-44]. He
emphasizes their union with the words tecum ("with
you") emphatically placed and repeated in lines 41-42,
unum opus ("a single task") and pariter ("equally")
contrasted with ambo ("the two of us") in line 43. He
sums it all up in astrological terms: astrology was
widely approved by educated people in Persius's time,
including Stoics, and it is frequently referred to in
contemporary literature. Persius imagines that he and
Cornutus, born under the benign influence of Libra (the
Scales) or Gemini (the Twins), are protected by Jupiter
against the hostile influence of Saturn. It was
believed that those born under Libra had a great capacity for friendship (6), while Gemini is an appropriate
sign for two people so closely united. Whatever the
astrological accuracy of Persius's words, he makes the
harmony between him and Cornutus clear by repetition of

words expressing constancy and union and, finally, by
translating the Greek idea of harmony into Latin in
line 51: "some star certainly brings me into harmony
with you" (me tibi temperat) (7).

Having thus explained his poetic and philosophical
foundations, Persius is ready at last to begin his
moral disquisition. Cornutus, as interlocutor, has
served his purpose. He makes a last appearance in
lines 62-64 where his devotion to philosophy is contrasted with the lusts and greed of other men. He is
there described as a farmer whose fields are the young,
which he clears of the weeds of error and sows with the
seeds of Stoic philosophy: "cultor enim iuvenum pur-
gatas inseris aures/fruge Cleanthea" ("For as a farmer
of young men you clear their ears and sow the seed of
Cleanthes"). This, says Persius, is the source of
wisdom of the journey of life for young and old alike
[lines 64-65], and, he implies, the Stoic teaching of
Cornutus will justify his own moral teaching, which is
so much at variance with the goals of the great majority of men, as described in lines 52-61. "What's the
hurry? Tomorrow is time enough," he imagines an interlocutor saying [lines 66-67], and he illustrates his
reply [lines 67-72] with a memorable and original metaphor: "However close to you the front-wheel's rim,
although you are under the same carriage you will never
catch it as it rolls along, since you run along as the
rear wheel on the rear axle." Time wasted can never be
caught up. Persius's metaphor vividly describes the
inexorable advance of time and the inability of the
individual to break out of its confinement.

Yet there is one way, philosophy, and now finally
Persius embarks on his diatribe on true freedom, in
which liberty is the first word. His preparation for
his diatribe appears long and indirect, as is appropriate to the conversational style of satire. Yet it
should not mislead the reader into supposing that the
satirist is not in control of his material. In three
"paragraphs" of roughly equal length he has set forth
the principles of his poetry and philosophy and acknowledged his debt to Cornutus. In the third he sets
Cornutus's and his own doctrines apart from the goals
of ordinary men, just as in the first he had distinguished himself from other poets and their audiences.
And in the last few lines [66-72] he prefaces the
diatribe by emphasizing the urgency of his theme.

These 72 lines, in sum, comprehend the principles and
major themes of Persius's work, while cast in the form
of a tribute to his friend and teacher. They are a
weighty preparation for his discussion of the Stoic
paradox "Only the wise are free."
     The diatribe falls into two broad sections of rough-
ly equal length. In the first [lines 73-131] the
general theme of liberty is set forth and the falsity
of the usual definition of freedom is established. In
the second [lines 132-88] a series of examples is given
to illustrate the theme of the first part.
     The first part revolves round the definition of
liberty. To most people it is the opposite of slavery
in the physical and legal sense, and Persius illustrates the common view with a vigorous account of the
manumission of the slave Dama (8) and his sudden trans-
formation into Marcus, a respectable Roman citizen
[lines 73-82]. This is what people call real freedom.
"All right, then," replies an interlocutor [lines 83-
85], "what about the man who lives just as he likes?
Isn't he truly free?" The interlocutor is using the
Stoics' own words, for they said that "freedom was to
live as one wished," with the necessary premise (here
ignored by the interlocutor) that wishes are based on
knowledge. Therefore knowledge of what is right must
precede right exercise of the will. It follows that
only he who knows what is right (that is, the wise man)
is free to make right choices. The ordinary man
(represented here by the interlocutor) thinks he has
freedom of choice and is therefore more free than the
early Roman hero Brutus, who drove out the tyrants
[lines 84-85]. In reality, he is still a slave to his
passions, because he does not have the knowledge to
make the right moral choices. Persius skillfully puts
the Stoic words into the interlocutor's mouth, but it
is easy for him to point out the deficiencies in his
opponent's syllogism (mendose colligis ["your syllogism
is false," line 85]). Here he speaks as a Stoic "whose
ears have been rinsed with sharp vinegar" [lines 85-
87], an echo of line 63 where Cornutus had "cleared
young men's ears to plant Stoic seed." First, he says,
you are not able to choose ("'licet' illud et 'ut volo'
tolle" ["take away the words 'I can' and 'as I
like'"]). To confuse becoming a freedman (that is, ex-
slave) with being morally free reflects an old
misconception: "I will pull the old grandmothers out

of your heart" [line 92] is Persius's colorful expression. Persius then shows how moral decisions need a trained mind [lines 93-108]: the magistrate who frees the slave cannot give him the fine moral sense to make difficult decisions amid the hurry of life, no more than an untrained laborer can instantly become a concert pianist. That is a matter of common sense and it is, he maintains, a natural law that ignorance prevents people from doing jobs that need training. This is the case with doctors or sea-captains: just so one needs education to recognize true from false, as much in ethics as with coins.

Persius continues [lines 109-23]: "Suppose you outwardly keep all the conventions of good behavior and ignore the temptations of greed and truly know what limit to set to your acquisitions. Then I will grant you are free." But if "you still keep the cunning fox lurking in your sour heart" [line 117], then even that concession must be withdrawn, for even the most trivial action will prove your lack of moral training. And finally [124-31], as the interlocutor feebly replies, "But I am a free man," Persius proves that the inner desires and passions are just as much tyrants as are a slave's master with his harsh orders. The interlocutor, untrained in philosophy, is as much a slave to his passions as the slave to his master.

This long section [lines 73-131] proceeds in the conversational manner appropriate to the principles of satiric composition that Persius has established in the first twenty lines of the poem. Gnomic utterances (for example, lines 96-99) alternate with vivid examples (for example, lines 76-81, 122-23); philosophical diatribe is enlivened by dialogue, metaphorical usages, and variation of style and vocabulary. In style the passage is an example of "clever juxtaposition of ordinary Romans' words" used for a moral purpose, exactly as Persius has described in lines 14-16. The philosophic message is the result of Cornutus's training, and so the passage bears out the description of Persius's moral training that has been set forth in lines 30-40. The continuous forward movement of the satire, in accordance with Persius's planned structure, is evident, despite the apparent indirection of the satiric style.

For the rest of the diatribe [lines 132-188] Persius illustrates his thesis (that only the wise man is free)

by examples of "passions" (to use the Stoic term) that
keep the non-Stoic enslaved. First come Avarice and
Luxury, twin mistresses who pull their victim in
different directions [lines 132-60]. Avarice, personified, wakes up her sleeping victim and urges him to
turn to and make a voyage to the East in search of trade
and profit. Just as he is ready to set sail, Luxury
appears and equally persuasively urges him to stay and
enjoy the pleasures of life at home. So the wretched
man is torn between the two, for he is a slave to both.
Even if he succeeds in resisting one or the other he
cannot be free, for he is like a dog that breaks its
chain yet drags a length of the chain with it as it
runs away.

Another example of a man who is a slave to the
passions is the young man in love [lines 61-75].
Here Persius adapts a scene from Menander's comedy
Eunuchus (9). The young lover has decided to give up
his pursuit of the girl; ironically, his adviser and
source of wisdom is his slave, Davus. But then he
thinks: "Suppose she asks me to come back? Should I
go?" Davus's reply amounts to "all or nothing": "if
you left her completely and left no part of you behind,
not even now (that is, when she invites you) should you
go." Emphasis is on completeness, and Persius draws
the conclusion: "here, in this slave, is the free man
we are looking for, not in the meaningless ceremony of
giving a slave his freedom."

At this stage Persius has completed his diatribe and
has established his thesis. He does, however, add two
further examples, of the man enslaved by ambition and
running for political office [176-79], and of the man
who is at the mercy of superstitions [lines 179-88],
among which Persius singles out the cults of the Jews,
of Cybele, and of Isis, as well as ignorant Roman
superstitions. It is a lively glimpse of the multipli-
city of religions in imperial Rome, but the passage,
for all its vividness, does not add anything new to the
diatribe.

A three-line epilogue [lines 189-91] brings the
satire to an end on an ironic note. A burly centurion
(10), representing the ignorant majority of ordinary
Romans, laughs coarsely and offers a clipped 100-cent
coin for a hundred Greek philosophers. Besides the
structural function of linking the figure 100 to the
opening lines of the satire, the passage leaves the

satirist alone, independent of the masses, as he had promised in lines 19-21. His message, however true, is still only for the few who have ears to hear.

The fifth satire is the most ambitious of Persius's poems and has generally been considered his masterpiece. However, it has also been criticized for lack of coherent structure, for a certain preciosity in the eulogy of Cornutus, and for a lack of quality in the moral diatribe. We have seen that the satire does have its own coherence and particularly that the opening fifty-two lines (which include the eulogy) relate to what follows. The nature of Persius's friendship with Cornutus can only be judged subjectively, and Persius gives few details of how Cornutus actually taught. His purpose is rather to establish a sufficiently strong foundation in this satire upon which to build his moral diatribe.

The question of the quality of Persius's moralizing is harder to decide. By comparison with the diatribe of Epictetus (no. 4) on the same subject Persius lacks the force that comes with experience. Nor does he convey the bitter anger of Juvenal in his depiction of vice. Since these authors were writing some forty or more years after Persius's death and for different audiences, it is questionable whether any meaningful comparison can be made along these lines. It is more instructive to look back in time from Persius and consider how he compares with Horace. Like every other satirist until Boileau and Pope, he does not match Horace in urbanity and ironic wit. This said, there remain ample grounds for a comparison. The fifth satire is on the same theme as the seventh of Horace's second book, and its use of a diatribe within a conversation is similar to Horace's third satire of the second book, which is also on the theme of a Stoic paradox. There are more direct imitations of Horace in this satire than any other: of the forty-eight imitative passages analyzed by a recent German scholar no less than nineteen come from the fifth satire (11). It is obvious that Persius was especially conscious of emulating Horace in this satire. He was putting his own stamp on a subject already so well-known that an absolutely original treatment was no longer possible. Persius makes no concealment of his debt to Horace-- indeed, the conventions of __aemulatio__ ("literary imitation") at Rome required that the audience recognize the

sources of the imitative passages and judge the poet
for the skill with which he transmuted his model. We
can be less sure of the extent of his emulation of
Lucilius in this satire, but his words in lines 14-16
show that his aim was to be closer to the skillful
juxtaposition of words and the understated wit of Horace
than to the outspoken social and moral criticism of
Lucilius (to which he refers in lines 114-15 of the
first satire). He claims "to scrape vice" (radere
mores, line 5.15; the same verb is used at 1.107) and
to do this with "gentlemanly well-educated wit" (ingenuo
ludo) and these phrases, taken with secrete loquimur
(line 21; "my words are for a private audience"),
define clearly enough the limits that Persius set for
himself. His special achievement in this satire lies
in the skillfully constructed phrases and the close-
packed metaphors. His description of his poetic principles is a fine piece of literary criticism in its own
right, and the personal statement to Cornutus allows
the satirist to adopt a persona whose sincerity justifies the subsequent moral diatribe. Above all, it is
the vigorous language that marks the satire out. The
metaphors abound: the twisted branches of a beech-tree
for an inveterate gambler's fingers, the individual as
the back wheel of a wagon caught in the inexorable
advance of time, the "old grandmothers" of prejudice in
a man's mind, the cunning fox in the unreformed sinner's
heart--these are just a few of the poetic phrases that
mark Persius's originality. He succeeds in achieving
exactly what he sets out to do in presenting the well-
known Stoic paradox to a select audience.

The Sixth Satire

The satiric program described by Persius in the
first satire is complete by the end of the fifth. His
main themes are poetic style and morality, and the
inseparable union between them. In the fifth satire
Cornutus represents the good man in both literary and
moral senses, and Persius, as his close friend and
pupil, puts himself forward as a second exemplar,
delivering a moral diatribe in the appropriate satiric
style. His moral thesis, that only the wise man (that
is, the Stoic philosopher) is free, is the goal toward
which the moral criticism of the earlier satires has

been proceeding. It is therefore neither necessary nor desirable to include the sixth satire in the structure of the body of Persius's book. It is rather in the nature of an epilogue, in which the poet retreats from the uncompromising Stoic austerity of the earlier satires and speaks to a friend through a more relaxed persona.

It seems that the unique position of the sixth satire caused doubts in antiquity, for we find in the ancient Life of Persius, the following: "He left this very book incomplete. Some lines have been removed from the end of it to make it look as if it had been finished. Cornutus slightly shortened it, and handed it over to Caesius Bassus, at his request, for publication."

These words raise many problems: for example, was the sixth satire left unfinished, or did Persius start a seventh, which was then removed by Cornutus? To what extent did Cornutus shorten the book, and was he concerned chiefly with editing just the sixth satire? The most probable answers are that Persius did not live to put the final touches on the sixth satire, and that Cornutus removed some material from the end while changing as little as he could from Persius's draft. This would explain the abruptness of the ending and the presence of some obscure passages that might well have been revised had Persius lived to finish his work. Cornutus preferred to leave the poem as far as possible in the form that Persius had left it.

The satire is in the form of a letter to Caesius Bassus and it has rightly been called the most Horatian of Persius's satires. Horace's first book of Epistles deals with literary, social, and ethical questions in an informal style, each poem being addressed to a friend. The style and meter are the same as for the Satires, and the persona adopted by Horace is invariably relaxed and affable. Nowhere is this clearer than in the brief letter [Epistle 1.4] addressed to the elegiac poet Albius Tibullus. Horace imagines what his friend is doing in northern Italy--is he writing poetry or enjoying solitary walks in the countryside thinking about things "that are worthy of a wise and good man"? At the end Horace reverts to himself with typical self-irony: "You will see me plump and sleek, with skin well cared-for, when you want to laugh, a pig from the sty of Epicurus" (Epicuri de grege porcum). By his repetition of the word curare ("to care for") applied first to the philosophical thoughts of Tibullus and then to his own physical appearance, Horace underlines the contrast between the serious issues of ethics and the life of moderate pleasures, and does it with such a smiling self-irony, that, as we leave the poem, we can be sure that Horace, too, cares about the former even while enjoying the Epicurean life.

This letter is the model for Persius's sixth satire, while its successor [Epistle 1.5] provides Persius with material upon which to pattern his diatribe on the proper use of one's material goods. "What is the point of having a fortune," says Horace [Epistle 1.5.12-15], "if I am not allowed to spend it? The man who is frugal because he worries about his heir and is too austere is next to a madman. I will begin to drink and scatter flowers, I will even allow myself to be considered a fool."

These two Horatian passages give Persius his framework. In the fifth satire he had been the uncompromising Stoic preaching an austere way of life. In the sixth his persona is more genial and closer to the Epicureanism of Horace. The two main principles of the Epicurean way of life were moderation--summed up in Horace's famous phrase aurea mediocritas, "the golden mean," and the avoidance of pain (12). The principle of the "middle way" is similar to the Stoics' principle of the avoidance of the passions, and it prevented the avoidance of pain from becoming an excuse for hedonism. Persius is not therefore unreasonably inconsistent in adopting an Epicurean point of view in the sixth satire, and we should remember that the ancient Life, in telling of Persius's friendship with Cornutus, says only that "he made some progress in philosophy," words that could hardly be applied to an uncompromising Stoic. The mild touch of Horatian Epicureanism in the persona of the sixth satire should not come as a surprise.

The satire falls into three parts, an introduction, lines 1-24, a diatribe, lines 25-74, and an epilogue, lines 75-80. In structure it is similar to the second satire, which also begins with a personal address to a friend [lines 1-5] and is followed by a diatribe [lines 6-75]. In the sixth, however, the introduction is longer and more complex: in particular, the passage from lines 12-24 serves the function of uniting the two parts and achieves a coherence that is evidence for Persius's increasing mastery of the techniques of satire.

In lines 1-6 he addresses Caesius Bassus. It is wintertime, the time for indoor activities, sitting by the fire, composing lyric poetry. Persius subtly compliments Bassus on his metrical skill and his achievement (reminiscent of Horace's well-known boast at the end of his third book of Odes) in adapting Greek lyric meter and music to the language of Roman poetry. The phrase "veterum primordia vocum" ("the first beginnings of ancient sounds," line 3) intentionally recalls Lucretius, the great Epicurean epic poet, who died in 55 B.C. Lucretius had emphasized the difficulty of his task in adapting Greek philosophical concepts to the Latin language, and the phrase primordia rerum (literally "the first beginnings of things") is his equivalent of the Greek word atoma. So Persius imagines Bassus taking the ancient Latin words and unconnected musical notes, and bringing them into the harmonious creation of Latin lyric poetry (13). Moreover, he describes the sound of the "Latin lyre" as virile (marem), both contrasting it with the smoothness of Greek lyric and reminding the reader of his strictures against the effeminate poetry of his contemporaries in the first satire. Finally, Persius imagines Bassus composing lyrics on the different themes that since the time of Pindar (fifth century B.C.) had been canonical in Greek and Roman criticism. These are succinctly given in Horace's Ars Poetica, lines 83-85: "The Muse granted to the lyre to tell of the gods and the sons of gods, the winners in boxing and horse-racing, of the anxieties of the young and of liberating wine." Bassus, though past his youth (senex, line 6, in emphatic position), gives attention to the lighter themes of love and wine: "[skilled] . . . next at dealing with the laughter of the young, and yourself a fine old man skilled at writing on lighter themes."

Like Cornutus in satire 5 and Macrinus in satire 2, Bassus is an older friend whom Persius first compliments and then makes the recipient of a diatribe. The complex address to Bassus has an integral part in the satire. It contrasts the older man with Persius himself--indeed, the emphatic senex in line 6 is followed immediately by mihi; the compact survey of the genre of Latin lyric poetry in lines 2-6 links the satire to

Horace, the greatest of Latin lyric poets as well as
Persius's model in satire; the lighter love-lyrics of
Bassus (the word lusisse in line 6 literally means "to
have played") are contrasted with the serious moral
diatribe of the satirist that is to come.
Having prepared the stage, the satirist himself then
steps forward: "As for me, I'm spending a mild winter
on the Ligurian coast with my own patch of sea." The
geographical reference allows him to quote a line from
Ennius [line 9], written, Persius says, after "he had
given up his dream of being Homer," that is, in a
different poem from his great epic, the Annales (14).
Thus Persius still separates himself from the genre of
epic, as he had done in his prologue to the Satires.
Lines 12-24 form the third part of this complex
introduction. The Epicurean Lucretius had likened
himself to a man looking from dry land at the stormy
seas and shipwrecks. Similarly, Persius used his
peaceful winter retreat as an allegory for a self-
sufficient philosophy of life, which is founded upon
freedom from the passions of fear, jealousy, and avarice [lines 12-17]. He grants [lines 18-22] that
others may differ; even of those who were born under
the same sign of the Zodiac, one may be a miser, the
other a spendthrift. Persius's own position is in the
middle, and he announces his choice of the Golden Mean
by appropriately quoting from Horace (15). Horace had
said that the individual's "Genius," which he defines
as "the companion who regulates the star of one's
birth," knows each person's nature Then he continues:
"I shall use my goods, and I shall take from my
moderate heap as much as the circumstances demand; nor
shall I fear what my heir thinks of me because he does
not find more than I inherited. Yet I would also like
to know the same thing--how far different is the frank
and cheerful person from my grandson, and how far is
the frugal person at odds with the miser."
The underlined words--respectively utar, acervo,
discrepet--are all used significantly by Persius
(respectively in lines 22, 80, 18) and the ideas of the
Horatian passage are all interwoven in his poem.
Therefore when he announces his choice of the Golden
Mean with the repeated word utar--utar ego, utar, his
hearers immediately associate the lines with the Horatian context. The idea of the "moderate heap" is more
literally used by Persius in the image of the harvest

[lines 25-26]: "live to the limit of your harvest and grind your store of grain, for it is right. Why should you hesitate? Break up the earth, and a second crop is green."

Let us review the twenty-four lines of introduction. Persius puts his satire in the form of a letter to an older friend, whose poetry is of a different genre from his own. With passing allusions to Ennius and Lucretius, he elaborately establishes his debt to Horace, whose principle of the Golden Mean and of moderate enjoyment of good things in the present is the basis of Persius's stance. Finally, he announces the theme of his diatribe, which is the proper use of money.

The fifty-six lines of the diatribe [25-80] start with a statement of the theme in lines 25-26 (quoted above), in which Horace's _acervus_ ("heap") is paraphrased in the metaphor of the harvest and the granary. Quite apart from the poetic qualities of these lines, Persius's paraphrase is effective because his hearers, familiar with the passage in Horace (as they certainly were), would know Horace's original phrase, _ex modico acervo_ ("from a moderate heap"). Persius waits until the last word in the satire to use the word _acervus_ [line 80], thus establishing a ring composition for his diatribe and giving full significance to the Horatian concept of the "heap" (that is, one's capital), but used in the end by Persius in a Stoic context, as we shall see.

Immediately (to return to the start of the diatribe) an objection is raised [lines 27-33]. "I need to use my capital to help a shipwrecked friend." "Fine," replies the satirist, "break off some of your land and give it to your destitute friend." This leads to a second objection: the satirist's heir will be angry if his inherited capital is reduced by such generosity [lines 33-36], and he will not even give his benefactor a decent funeral. Moreover [lines 37-40], he has the support of "Mr. Beastly" (Bestius), who speaks for the average conservative Roman: "You can blame this sort of thing on the new-fangled ideas introduced by the clever Greeks, which are giving the Roman laborer tastes above his station" (16).

At this point, halfway through the poem, the satirist takes his heir aside from crowd, as if to remind him of principles that are too fine for vulgar people like Bestius. He imagines that a national holiday has

been announced to celebrate the victory of the Emperor
Gaius (Caligula, who reigned 37-41) over the Germans
[lines 43-47]. It is quite in keeping with Roman
satiric conventions to take an example from an earlier
time (indeed, forty years later Juvenal made this a
cardinal principle of his satiric technique, most probably making a virtue of necessity in a repressive
age), and Persius adds a pleasant flavor of irony by
using a triumph that was false, to celebrate a victory
that never was won (17). A public holiday?--the satirist must do his bit for the national celebration. He
will give a gladiatorial show with one hundred pairs
of fighters and distribute free oil, bread, and meat
for the people. (In his enthusiasm the satirist has
for the moment lost sight of Horace's "moderate heap":
the public munificence of lines 48-51 would be beyond
the means of one with modest capital. The irony is
intentional.) Seeing his heir's disapproving expression, he invites him to say what he thinks loud and
clear, for all to hear, an invitation which, if accepted, will certainly lead the people to stone the
heir for trying to stop their enjoyment (18). "Very
well," replies the satirist to the heir's refusal, "I
will find myself another heir, a 'son of the earth'
[lines 52-60]: we are all related if you go back a few
generations, so this beggar I pick up from the main
road south of Rome probably has just as good a claim as
you, my immediate but recalcitrant heir."
     Now the satirist returns more directly to his point.
Using the metaphor of a relay-race, he asks why the
heir will not let him finish his "leg" of the race:
after all, the satirist is like the god Mercury, the
god of luck and lucky increases in wealth, painted by
artists with a full purse. Even the prospect of the
outright gift of the legacy will not satisfy the heir,
who complains that something is missing. "Yes,"
admits the satirist, "I spent it for my own purposes,
and don't try to balance the account of what is left."
And with that the satirist gives up on the heir. Returning to his imaginary feast (possibly still the one
celebrating Caligula's victory, but more likely now to
be an unspecified occasion), he orders his servant to
pour on expensive condiments: why should he, like a
miser, dine off nettles and half a smoked pig's head,
and reduce himself to skin and bones, just for the
benefit of a fat and sensual heir [lines 61-74]?

The main part of the diatribe is ended, and it remains for the satirist to point the moral in a brief epilogue [lines 75-80]. Returning to the theme of the introduction, he shows that it is greed that is the cause of the heir's impatience. In other words, the heir represents avarice, the satirist moderation, and there can be no common ground. In the introduction to the satire, Persius is free from anxiety and envy, not driven by avarice to drink sour wine [lines 12-17]. In the epilogue he imagines the interlocutor (probably no longer anyone as specific as the heir or Bassus) bartering his life for profit, trading in every corner of the world, doubling his capital again and again. Even when he has increased it ten times, he will not know when to stop, and the satire ends with him saying: "Tell me when to stop; Chrysippus, the person has been found who can complete your heap." In other words, his greed is limitless, because Chrysippus's problem is insoluble (19).

Persius's use of the <u>acervus</u> ("heap") to end his satire is brilliant, linking the Stoic paradox to the theme of Epicurean moderation with which the diatribe had begun [lines 25-26]. There, as we have seen, Persius paraphrased Horace's use of the word <u>acervus</u> by using the metaphor of harvest and granary. His reason for doing this becomes clear at line 80. The pessimistic conclusion is the more pointed for the allusion to the well-known riddle of Chrysippus's heap. Persius ends on a Stoic note, while gracefully acknowledging his debt to Horace, and at the same time he achieves a well-rounded structure for the satire.

Yet there is one final irony, which again links the ending to the introduction. There is one person, in fact, who has solved Chrysippus's problem--the satirist. The heir, representing greed, and "Mr. Beastly," representing meanness, are the common people, liable to these extremes of "passion" (to use the Stoic term for the Greek word <u>pathos</u>). Only the wise man knows how to take the middle road of the Golden Mean, and Persius has already claimed this territory for himself in lines 12-24. Especially significant is the phrase <u>securus vulgi</u> [line 12], "not worried about the crowd." Once again, as in the first and fifth satires, the satirist emerges at the end as a solitary figure, independent of the prejudices and weaknesses of the common crowd, capable of achieving the good and moderate life because

he has through philosophy achieved wisdom. Finally, to
soften the harshness of this somewhat priggish self-
satisfaction, Persius shows that he (as opposed to his
satirical persona) is capable of friendship and warm
humanity by the mellow tone of the satire's opening as
he addresses the epistle to his old friend Bassus.

So ends Persius's slender volume of satires. The
sixth satire in a way points to new developments in
Persius's art, analogous to the experience of Horace
himself. After writing satires in the Lucilian tradition, Horace turned to the verse epistle, in which he
addressed letters to his friends, each dealing with a
specific ethical or moral topic. As we have seen,
Persius's satirical program was complete with the fifth
satire, while the sixth is closer to the Epistles of
Horace in technique, content, and tone. On the other
hand, there is no loss of satiric force or poetic
skill. The sixth satire is rich in metaphor and example; it exhibits a lively use of satiric dialogue and
sketches the vivid scene (for example, the shipwrecked
friend, or Caligula's triumph) as brilliantly as ever.
Its undoubtedly obscure passages (lines 3-4, 38-40, 51-
52 especially) may perhaps be attributable to Persius's
death before final revision could be completed. Over-
all, the satire shows the increasing maturity of the
poet and his mastery of the techniques of Horatian
satire.

Chapter Six
The Style of Persius

General Considerations

Style is inseparable from moral values. This is the theme of Persius's first satire, and it is the foundation of the fifth. For the satirist how he expresses himself is integral with what he says. The foregoing survey of the six satires has therefore involved many observations on Persius's style in passing; we may now turn our attention to it both for its own sake and as an instrument for Persius's expression of his character and moral teaching. Persius himself says a good deal about satirical style, especially in the prologue, the first, and the fifth satires, and it is with these that we shall be especially concerned.

Persius has the reputation of being obscure and difficult. In the fifth century the Byzantine scholar John of Lydia found him the "darkest" of writers (the Greek word is amauros), and critics have consistently dismissed him as inferior to Horace and Juvenal because of his close-packed metaphors, his strained diction, and his "scabrous and hobbling" verse (1). Some critics patronizingly excuse Persius on the grounds of youth and inexperience, and comparatively few have been generous or patient enough to consider his satire in its integrity, that is, to concentrate as much on the quality of his poetry as a whole as on its component parts. Kenneth Reckford, with a metaphor worthy of Persius himself, has rightly said: "to regard his metaphors as poetic embellishment leads to an unrewarding peeling away of onionskins: those who find nothing within need blame only themselves" (2).

The most persuasive defender of Persius was also his greatest editor, Isaac Casaubon, whose edition was published in Paris in 1605. Casaubon's Prolegomena to his edition are admittedly so biased as to dismiss the very real difficulties of Persius's style and were easily attacked by Dryden in his Discourse concerning the Original and Progress of Satire. Yet Casaubon was right to refuse to distinguish between style and content, and any consideration of Persius's style should

recognize the value of Casaubon's approach. He begins
with a broad definition of the principal constituent
parts of Roman satire, which he reduces to two: moral
instruction and wit (doctrina moralis, urbanitas et
sales). He finds that Persius excels in the former and
justifies his use of metaphor as being essential to the
creation of an appropriately lofty style, so that his
obscurity is incidental to the broader purpose of his
poetry. Casaubon fails, as Dryden pointed out, to
explain or justify Persius's obscurity, but his general
principles of criticism are correct.

In fact, the moral doctrines of Persius are neither
original nor arresting. To say, as he does, that sloth
or the passions are bad, or that prayer, to be acceptable to the gods, must come from a pure heart, is
hardly likely to excite one's hearers. But readers
since Persius's time have continually found his doctrines memorable because of the way in which he has
expressed them. A true poet can express the deepest
truths with a style that transforms the banal into the
memorable. When Horace chooses the simple and unob-
strusive life over that of the wealthy and powerful,
his doctrine is neither new nor exciting, but who can
fail to be moved by the picture of Fear and Threats
climbing to the top with the successful man, or of
black Care sailing on the merchant's ship and sitting
behind the horseman (3)?

Persius deals with a similar theme when he describes
the opposing tyrannies of avarice and luxury in Satire
5.132-60. Like Horace, he personifies the abstract
principles and dramatizes the dilemma of their victim.
He sets the scene: it is morning and the man is still
asleep. "Wake up!" cries Avarice and after some lively
dialogue prods him into preparing a boat with which to
import luxuries from the east. She advises him to
raise money for the venture, perjuring himself if necessary. All is made ready and the trader shouts "All
aboard!" when suddenly Luxury appears. "Where on earth
are you off to, you fool?" she cries. "Why put up with
the dangers and discomforts of a sea-voyage, when you
could stay here and enjoy yourself at ease? Why sweat
to double the return on your capital? Life is short:
relax and enjoy it!"

After this Persius typically adds his own commentary by means of two more concrete metaphors. The
businessman is pulled in opposite directions by two

hooks. When he has for once decided to resist one or the other vice, he is still like a chained dog that escapes, yet drags part of the chain with him.

The whole passage is an elaboration on a very simple theme--the conflicting temptations of greed and sloth. By means of lively dialogue, personifications and direct address, vignettes of dockside scenes and shipboard life, Persius brings to life the basic moral doctrine of his diatribe that only the wise man is free. By the closing image of the chained dog he gives a final, concrete immediacy to the moral servitude of the businessman, who is no more free than the chained animal.

How obscure is this passage? In outline and purpose it is simple. It is made harder by the swift-moving dialogue with frequent changes of speaker; by the kaleidoscopic changes of scene from bedroom, to dockside, to ship, and back to land again; by complex descriptions of psychological states; by technical or unusual words (for example, the archaic obba for a wine jar); finally by the changing series of concrete images: the snoring businessman; the eastern merchandise; the honest man doing no more with his life than licking salt from his fingers and happy to be so poor; the scenes of loading the boat; the imagined shipboard meal taken on deck as the businessman props himself up on a coil of rope; the sour wine that the sailor drinks; the vision of the short life to be enjoyed; the two hooks; the broken chain and the dog. In less than thirty lines there are a dozen concrete images, and this passage is by no means exceptional.

The passage that we have been examining [Satire 5.132-60] is quite representative of Persius's style, and it contains many of the elements that distinguish him from other satirists. Before we consider these in greater detail, we should remind ourselves of the state of the tradition of Latin hexameter satire when Persius began to write. The most obvious consideration is the revolution achieved by Horace. As J. P. Sullivan has aptly said: "Horace . . . succeeded in reducing a fairly free form, free in terms both of subject and language, into a smooth conversational musing" (4). The satirist, as we have seen, derived his style in part from comedy and diatribe. Lucilius had brought to these Greek genres his own forceful indignation and a flexible range of subject matter, style, and vocabulary.

Horace disciplined the vigorous but comparatively
informal qualities of Lucilian satire. In place of
abuse, indignation, obscenity, and laughter, he chose
the subtler weapons of irony and wit; in place of the
frontal attack he chose indirection, speaking through
the mask of a subtly changing persona. These methods
suited both his character (as far as he ever permits us
to see it behind the mask) and his social and political
circumstances.

A century later Persius tells us how he perceives
his predecessors: "Lucilius cut up the city--you,
Lupus, and you, Mucius--and broke his teeth on them.
Horace, the rogue, touches every fault in his smiling
friend; allowed entry, he plays around the inmost
heart, cleverly suspending his public from his fasti-
diously critical nose" [Satire 1.114-18].

Persius then goes on to admit that he cannot use the
indignation of Lucilius and to imply (though he does
not say so explicitly) that he will not rival Horace in
wit and subtle charm. At the same time he will, he
says, uncover the vices of Roman society (as his
predecessors had done) by talking, as it were,
privately. He uses the images of Midas's barber dig-
ging the hole into which to whisper his discoveries of
Rome's secret vices [Satire 1.119-23], but he knows
also that these private musings will be heard by
others. His "public" he has already defined [Satire
1.3] as "one or two people," and he describes them now
as discriminating, familiar with the candor of the Greek
comic poets and capable of appreciating satire that is
more refined. Persius's style, therefore, is to be
subtle and personal. It neither states the obvious
nor, to put it his way [Satire 1.127-33], can it be
understood by the lout who laughs at the one-eyed man
for being one-eyed. He sums it up in the fifth satire:
"secrete loquimur" ("we talk privately," line 21).

But Persius cannot ignore Horace's achievement in
making satire conversational, as implied by Horace's
title of Sermones ("talks") for his satires. In the
prologue Persius says that his work is not to be ranked
as poetry with the divinely inspired and lofty genres
of epic, tragedy, and lyric. Nor (he implies) will he
be a merely imitative versifier, writing for money. His
poetry (carmen nostrum, line 7) is the work of a semi-
initiate into the mysteries of poetry, a kind of halfway member (semipaganus) of the guild of poets. In

other words, he recognizes the conversational (as opposed to poetic) quality of Horatian satire as an essential part of the tradition. In the first satire he distances himself from the bombast and froth of contemporary poetry, notably epic and tragedy: he sees the rottenness of the literary products in vogue as manifestations of the moral rottenness of Roman society.

We can now outline the problems that Persius faced in developing his satiric style. Like Horace he needed to be conversational yet subtle; like Lucilius he aimed to be critical of the vices of society. Like any poet worth the name he needed technical skill. He wished to appeal to a discriminating audience. Finally, he intended to be honest, true to his moral and artistic principles. In the first satire he staked out his position as a literary and moral critic while in the fifth he explained the making of his style, forged in the fire of Cornutus's teaching [Satire 5.1-29]. A few lines from the latter passage [Satire 5.14-16] are the best summary of Persius's own view of his style (Cornutus is the speaker):

> verba togae sequeris iunctura callidus acri,
> ore teres modico, pallentis radere mores
> doctus et ingenuo culpam defigere ludo.

"You keep to the words of ordinary Romans; you are skillful with the telling, pointed juxtaposition; your well-rounded speech is not high-flown. You are skilled at scraping away sickly bad habits and at pinning guilt with a gentleman's wit."

Vocabulary

There are just short of two thousand different words used by Persius (1,938 out of 4,647 total words). No less than 1,237 (or 63.8 percent) of these are used once only, a sure indicator of the variety of Persius's language (5). The great majority of words are _verba togae_, ordinary words, that would not be out of place in prose speech. Equally, very few are words peculiar to the "lofty" styles of epic, tragedy, or lyric, and these are to be found in parodies of those styles, especially at the beginnings of the first and fifth

satires. The first line of satire 1 is instructive:
the word _inane_ ("empty," "vain") has the epic associations of Lucretius's poem _De Rerum Natura_, and the
exclamation is both a parody of the epic and philosophic style and a statement of the satirist's own negative feelings about the world he observes. The latter
is emphasized by Casaubon, who devotes four pages of
commentary to the line; the former is underlined by the
immediate interruption of the interlocutor, who pricks
the bubble of bombast with "who will read this sort of
stuff?" The skillful use of the single word _inane_, in
the emphatic last position in the first line of the
satire, is a microcosm of Persius's care in the choice,
placing, and associations of his words.

Persius again uses epic diction and vocabulary in
Satire 1.93-102, where he is parodying contemporary
epic effusions, and in 5.1-4, where the context and
purpose are quite similar to the opening of the first
satire. In the latter passage the interlocutor (Cornutus himself) again breaks in impatiently to stop the
high-flown bombast. He in turn uses epic parody in line
7: "grande locuturi nebulas Helicone legunto" ("let
those who will speak in the lofty style gather clouds
from Mount Helicon"). The parody lies not only in the
sense but also with the quasi-legal imperative _legunto_
(6), and the heavy epic rhythm of _locuturi_ before the
caesura. We have already noted Persius's exact use of
epic-philosophical vocabulary in line 3 of satire 6,
where the Lucretian phrase "veterum primordia rerum"
("first beginnings of ancient sounds") is used in describing the creation of a new lyric style by Caesius
Bassus.

Amongst the _verba togae_ ("words of ordinary
Romans") Persius uses many words appropriate to everyday speech and unsuitable for the poetry of epic or
tragedy. This very fact makes the words seem difficult
to us, because our reading of Latin is confined mostly
to literary works that exclude "vulgar" words (7). Yet
the words themselves were not necessarily rare or
abstruse. An analogy in English might be words such as
"businessman," "carburetor," "hamburger." These three
words are common enough in three major areas of re-
ference--respectively, daily work, technical terms,
eating--but they would not normally appear in poetic
contexts, except in parody, comic verse, or for particular effect in serious poetry, (for example, T. S.

Eliot's poetry of social criticism). So Persius uses *agaso* (5.76: "a stable-boy," compare Horace, *Satire* 2.8.72); *cerdo* (4.51: "a common workman"); *trossulus* (1.82: "a Roman nobleman," with pejorative overtones, as in Seneca, *Epistles*, 76.2 and 87.9). Among technical terms he uses *cannabis* (5.146: "a rope made of hemp"); *obba* (5.148: "a wine-jar," but already an archaic, although vulgar, word by Persius's time) (8); *orca* (3.50 and 76: "a narrow-necked jar," also used by Horace, *Satire* 2.4.66). Of our three areas of reference, eating provides the largest group of vulgar words, for example, *artocreas* (6.50: either "a meat-pie" or "a dish of bread and meat": the word, like many words in contemporary English usage, was coined from two greek words meaning respectively "bread" and "meat"); *perna* (3.75: "a ham": used also by Horace in *Satire* 2.2.117); *tuccetum* (2.42: "barbecued beef," said by the scholiast to be a term used by the Gauls of northern Italy for beef preserved in a special sauce).

So far we have been dealing only with substantives. With other parts of speech Persius is equally sensitive to the difference between the vocabulary of daily parlance and words appropriate to the lofty style of poetry. Adjectives appropriate to the latter appear in passages of epic parody, for example, *reparabilis* ("repetitive," in 1.102), or *inanis* ("empty," in 1.1) and *maestus* ("tragic," in 5.3). The epic word *grandis* ("vast") appears eight times, of which four are in passages critical of the turgid epic or rhetorical style [1.14, 68; 3.45; 5.7]; twice it is used in the context of food [2.42 and 3.55], each time with overtones of moral criticism (*fattening* porridge in 3.55; *gross* dishes in 2.42). At 5.186 the Galli (priests of Cybele) are *grandes*, size here being a sign of stupidity, just as three lines later [5.190] the vulgar and coarse man in the street, Pulfenius, is *ingens* ("huge"), another epic adjective. Finally, *grandis* is used at 6.22 for the vast estate which the spendthrift heir runs through. Persius's exactness with words is especially noticeable in this passage, in which he is alluding to Horace's description [*Epistle* 1.15.27] of another spendthrift who had exhausted his inheritance "heroically" (*fortiter*). Persius's spendthrift is a *magnanimus* . . . *puer* (lit. "a high-souled youth"), an epic phrase, for the virtue of *magnanimitas* (which is the Latin equivalent of the Greek *megalopsychia*) was especially appropriate to the epic hero, with its connotations of courage, nobility, and generosity. Further, Persius places the word next to grandia: "hic bona dente/grandia magnanimus peragit puer" ("here a generous youth runs through a vast fortune by chewing"), a collocation of words quite typical of Horace's style. Persius's words keep the style and associations of their Horatian model (9).

One group of adjectives peculiar to Persius includes those formed as past participles of verbs. There are more than twenty of these, and they add color and variety to Persius's style. Thus his reader's ear is vaporatus ("steamed") at 1.126. At 4.30-31, "tunicatum cum sale mordens/cepe et farratam pueris plaudentibus ollam . . ." ("nibbling on a salted onion, skin and all [lit. "clothed in its tunic"] and while his slaves applaud [the hand-out of] a bowl of grits [lit. "a bowl that has been 'gritted'"]"), the two participles humorously give a touch of grandeur that is quite incongruous with the rich skinflint and the plebeian food. At 1.125 (in the line preceding vaporatus) Persius forms a comparative adjective, from the participle decoctus, which means "boiled down," a metaphor from boiling away impurities during the making of wine. The comparative decoctius therefore intensifies the idea of something already free from fault and sets up the metaphor of vaporatus ("steamed") in the next line, to describe vividly the purity of Persius's literary standards.

As might be expected, Persius's verbs show an equally lively range, again with a careful distinction between those appropriate to the lofty style and those suitable for the sermo ("talk") of satire. The latter group, which is much larger, includes many drawn from everyday life or common speech. For example, the farming term runcare ("to pull weeds") is used at 4.36 of the homosexual removing body-hair, and the agricultural metaphor continues throughout the passage (through line 41), which, largely because of this device, is saved from being merely obscene. There are onomatopoeic verbs drawn from the children's nursery (lallare, "to say lalla" and pappare, "to cry for pap," 3.17-18.) In this passage Persius boldly uses the active infinitive forms of the verbs as substantives in his efforts to achieve poetic compression. Some verbs come directly from comedy: for example, the vivid

image of laughter behind one's back as the motion of
the stork's beak, imitated by the ridiculer's fingers,
is found first in Plautus (10). In Persius [1.58] the
verb pinsit ("opened and shut") introduces a brilliant
three-line passage in which the ridiculer's gestures
are likened to a catalog of animals--the stork's beak,
the donkey's ears, and the dog's tongue:

O Iane, a tergo quem nulla ciconia pinsit
nec manus auriculas imitari mobilis albas
nec linguae quantum sitiat canis Apula tantae.

"O Janus (sc. the two-faced god who could see behind
as well as in front), whom no stork "pecked" from
behind, nor the gesturing hand quick to imitate the
white ears (sc. of the donkey), nor tongues stuck
out as far as the thirsty Apulian dog's."

Persius's verbs are drawn from the whole range of
human activity and more than any other group of words
give vigor and color to his style. Trutinantur ("they
weigh in the scales," [3.82]) gives an exact picture,
in the centurion's scornful speech, of the pedantic
weighing of words indulged in by the professors of
philosophy. The scales, of course, are two pans sus-
pended from a beam, itself held up by the weigher; this
cumbersome process makes the transfer to the realm of
words all the more sarcastic, and the picture is made
yet more derisive by the exporrecto labello ("pursed
lips") of the professor. Many verbs are taken from
sexual and excretory functions, in keeping with the
element of obscentiy that had been part of the satiric
tradition from its Greek beginnings. Often Persius
adds an ironic or humorous twist. For example, to
describe subjects off-limits to the satirist's criticism, he imagines a picture of two serpents (such
pictures still exist, for example, at Pompeii) indica-
ting a sacred spot, and adds the comment: "pueri,
sacer est locus, extra meiite" ("boys, the place is
holy: piss elsewhere," 1.113). The simple use of the
incongruous term exactly and vividly catches both the
spirit and the predicament of the satirist. As a final
illustration of Persius's verbs we may choose the
expressive word bullire ("to boil, to send up bubbles
to the surface") and its compound ebullire ("to bubble
out [one's life]," that is, "to die"). In 3.32-34 the

atrophying of the moral sense of the spendthrift he-
donist is described as follows: "he is dull from his
vice and the rich fat has grown over his heart (sc. as
the seat of his thought); he has no conscience; he does
not know what he is losing, and sunk in the depths he
no longer sends up bubbles to the surface ("et alto/de-
mersus summa rursus non bullit in unda"). The single
word bullit vividly and exactly catches the sense of
the spendthrift as he sinks to the bottom, drowned in
his vices. Persius's choice of the one word bullit is
a masterpiece of poetic compression. It has philosophical connotations, for the image of the drowning man
was used by Greek and Roman moralists; taken literally
it is a vivid image. Finally, it neatly consummates
the moral atrophy whose progress has been described in
the previous phrases.

An important component of Persius's satiric vocabulary is the group of twenty-six diminutives (of which
nineteen are "true" diminutives as opposed to words
like puella ("a girl"), which are so common in the
diminutive form as not to be remarkable). Diminutives
are regularly formed by changing the substantive or
adjectival ending to -ellus (-a, -um) or -ulus: For
example, liber ("a book"), becomes libellus; rancidus
("sour"), becomes rancidulus. Latin, like modern
Italian, is extremely rich in diminutives, and they are
especially frequent in comedy and lyric poetry. The
soft -ll- sound is often used in passages of tender
emotion, often also with alliteration and other forms
of word-music. The connotations of smallness are most
often also exploited in passages of endearment, but
they are a rich source of vocabulary in passages expressive of scorn and derision, and at least half of
Persius's diminutives are used in this way. These
words invariably defeat the translator of Persius, for
English diminutives (the ending -ette, -kin, for example) seldom have the same connotations as Latin, and
there are no satisfactory parallels for diminutive
adjectives. Again, we find that Persius has exploited
the potential of Latin for poetic compression.

The most extended use of a diminutive is in the
first satire, where the word auricula (diminutive of
auris, "ear") is a significant motif in establishing
the unity of the poem. The diminutive is used for
scorn and disapproval. In its first appearance
[line 22] it is the means by which Romans "take in"

(literally and metaphorically) the degenerate poetry of
the day, and it is used at line 108 for the same purpose, where the hearers' "little ears" cannot accept
the biting criticism of the satirist. Twice the auriculae are the donkey's ears, imitated by the mocking
fingers in line 59, and with reference to the legend of
King Midas at line 121. In the latter passage Persius
finally gives the answer to the question he had left
incomplete at line 8: "Romae quis non . . . ?" ("Who
at Rome does not . . . ?"), answered in 121 by "auriculas asini quis non habet?" ("Who does not have the
little ears of the donkey?"). The intervening appear-
ances of the auriculae [lines 22, 59, 108] give the
word its necessary emphasis in 121 as well as contrib-
ute to the structural unity of the poem. The contrast
is all the more telling, therefore, when Persius uses
the nondiminutive auris in line 126, of the good
listener vaporata aure ("whose ear is well-steamed")
(11). Persius uses auricula once more in the second
satire [line 30] for the ears of the gods to whom
bribing prayers are offered. Here scorn for the
immoral petitioners is here transferred to the gods to
whom they pray.

Most of Persius's other diminutives are equally
colorful. Twice he uses pejorative diminutives for the
skin: in Satire 4.18 cuticula is used for the skin of
a specious candidate for political office tanning himself. Here, as with auricula and auris in satire 2,
Persius has the diminutive and nondiminutive words for
skin in close proximity avoiding the repetition (12).
Among Persius's other diminutives the following are
worth noting:

(1) Popellus (for populus, people) used pejorative-
ly twice at 4.15 and 6.50. Its synonym, plebecula (for
plebs) is used at 4.6, where it expresses scorn for the
instability of the mob. The association of the diminutive with comedy is especially noticeable here, since
Aristophanes had used the diminutive of demos
("people"), demidion (13).

(2) Persius coins the Greek form of the diminutive
elegidia ("little elegies") at 1.51 for the lightweight
verses of Roman noble poetasters.

(3) The diminutive aqualiculus (from aqualis,
"water-container") is an element in a deliberately
grotesque line at 1.57: "pinguis aqualiculus propenso
sesquipede extet" ("Your fat beer-belly hangs out half a

yard in front"). The diminutive for "stomach" is
appropriate, even in a context where large size is
emphasized, because it is pejorative, and the ungainly
word _aqualiculus_ suits the ponderous sound of the line
with its three polysyllabic words. The audience is
left no doubt as to what the satirist thinks of "beer-
bellies" (14).

(4) Persius uses six adjectival diminutives. For
example, _rancidulus_ ("sour") is used scornfully of the
poetic effusions of would-be amateur tragedians at
1.33. _Beatulus_, which also seems to be Persius's own
coinage from _beatus_ ("blessed"), is used at 3.103 of a
glutton who has eaten himself to death: "hinc tuba,
candelae, tandemque beatulus alto/compositus lecto . . ."
("hence the funeral trumpet and candles, and finally
the 'loved one' laid out on the high funeral bier . . .").
The diminutive adjective precisely catches the mixture
of hypocrisy in the mourners' emotions and the satirist's scorn.

This brief survey of Persius's vocabulary is necessarily selective, and it has not covered many important
elements in his choice of words--for example, Greek
words and constructions, archaic terms, neologisms, and
specially coined usages. Enough has been said, however, to give some idea of the richness and accuracy of
Persius's vocabulary, and the reader can judge how far
his claim to be using _verba togae_ ("words of ordinary
Romans") is justified. Single words can only give a
very partial idea of Persius's style, and it is appropriate now to turn to the most distinctive aspect of
his style, which he summarizes in the words "iunctura
callidus acri" ("skillful with the pointed juxtaposition"). His phrase (which is both an imitation of and
a compliment to Horace) (15) covers all aspects of his
weaving of words, the most important being his metaphorical language.

Metaphor

Metaphorical language is perhaps the most important
single feature of poetic writing. It achieves an immediacy and vividness that cannot be imparted by color-
less abstracts. It may be formalized, as in the
similes of epic, a feature of the grand style that is
clearly inappropriate to the _sermo_ of satire. There

are similes in Persius, but they are introduced inform-
ally, and the full epic formula of sicut (or ut: "just
as . . .") answered by haud aliter ("not otherwise . . .")
is not used. Persius twice uses a simile introduced by
ut (as): at 1.97 the critic of Vergil likens the
opening of the Aeneid to the branch of an old cork-tree
enveloped in a swollen bark, and in 6.62 the satirist
likens himself to the standard representation of Mercury, as the bringer of unexpected gain painted with a
wallet full of silver. Yet in this passage the point
of the simile (the purse) is not made explicitly.
Instead Persius indentifies himself with the god and,
by leaving the simile vague, achieves speed and compression: "Sum tibi Mercurius: venio deus huc ego ut
ille/pingitur" ("I am Mercury for you: I come here as
a god, just as he is painted"). There is also one
simile introduced by "non secus ac" ("no differently
than") at Satire 1.66.

Persius, therefore, like his predecessors, prefers
to use metaphorical writing as part of the onward flow
of his sermo; that is, he prefers image to simile.
This technique ensures speed and immediacy; it achieves
compression but often also increases obscurity. In the
Roman rhetorical handbooks the technique was called
translatio (an exact Latin equivalent for the Greek
metaphor), that is, the "carrying over" of a word or
phrase from one area of meaning to another. Its primary aim is vividness and therefore, as Cicero re-
marked, it is closely related to the senses, especially
the sense of sight (16). Thus it conveys abstract
ideas in concrete (usually visual) terms. Horace
exploited the richness of Latin imagery that Plautus
had first perceived and Lucilius developed. For example, he imagines men gossiping over the recent acquittal of an absent friend. One says: "he's a friend of
mine . . . but I do wonder how he got off" (17). The
satirist comments: "hic nigrae sucus lolliginis, haec
est/aerugo mera" ("This is the juice of the black
cuttlefish, this is unadulterated rust"). The black
and corrosive meanness of the false friend could not be
described more succinctly.

Horace perfected the technique of the callida
iunctura ("skillful joining") of words and phrases. He
seems to have coined the term iunctura, perhaps thinking of the metaphor of carpentry which underlines the
Greek word harmonia ("fitting together"). Horace used

callida iunctura in the context of giving freshness to
a well-used word. Persius's acris iunctura ("pointed
juxtaposition") introduces the notion of sharpness, the
Greek critical term being oxys. The English term
pointed is appropriate, since "point" is the essential
feature of wit, which is itself at the heart of satiric
technique. Persius's aim, therefore, was more ambitious than the goal implied by Horace's callida
iunctura, for it involved the achievement of surprise
and wit. The opposite of the term acris is tener
("soft"), precisely the quality in contemporary poetry
and its audience that Persius attacks in the first
satire (18). In contrast he aimed at poetry that was
spare and tense, its virile quality opposed to the
smooth effeminacy of his contemporaries. Here are his
comments at lines 63-66:

> What is the popular style? What else indeed except
> poems at last flowing along with soft meter, so that
> the smooth joints don't allow the critic's nails to
> find any roughness? The poet knows how to extend
> his verses just as if he were checking a red line's
> straightness with one eye.

Seneca, writing three years after Persius's death,
criticizes the "virile" quality of writers like Persius
who chose the pointed over the smooth style: "They
don't want their juxtapositions to be without roughness. They think it (sc. the juxtaposition) is virile
and heroic if it strikes the ear by its roughness"
(19).
So Persius's phrase acris iunctura ("pointed juxtaposition") is both descriptive and polemical. It
states his opposition to contemporary standards in
poetic taste, and it shows where his principal claim to
originality lies.
Let us now look at some specific examples. First
there are conjunctions of abstract and concrete that
are important for a whole passage or are so repeated
that they are significant elements in the structure of
the whole satire. In the first satire the ears are
used in this way, as we have already seen. It is
typical of Persius's style, however, that the physiological imagery of one part of the body (the ears) is
combined with that of others. Thus at 1.22 the poet
"collects tidbits for other men's ears," and the ears

become the means whereby the audience feed on bad poetry (a metaphor of digestion) and obtain sensual gratification (a metaphor of sexual perversion, lines 19-21). In this same passage the hearers' skin is swollen by the poetry they listen to (a metaphor of disease, in this case dropsy). In the lines immediately following [24-25] the interlocutor picks up on the idea of the body swelling and describes the urge to write bad poetry as fermentum ("yeast") and as a fig-tree that must "burst the heart and push itself outside." In the space of seven lines Persius has taken his basic image, the ears, and combined it with metaphors of sexual gratification, eating, disease, cooking, and trees. The passage is a good example of Persius's metaphorical writing. Johnson's strictures on the metaphysical poet Cowley are a relevant, although not altogether just, commentary:

> Wit . . . may be more rigorously and philosophically considered as a kind of discordia concors ("harmonious disharmony"); a combination of dissimilar images. . . . Of wit, thus defined they (that is, Cowley and those who wrote like him) have more than enough. The most heterogeneous ideas are yoked by violence together; . . . the reader . . . , though he sometimes admires, is seldom pleased. (20)

Nor is this all: returning to the recitations of bad poets [lines 32-35], the satirist describes the poet as "straining" the words (eliquat: a metaphor from crushing a grape and filtering its juice) and "tripping them up" (subplantat: a metaphor from wrestling) by his affected pronunciation. Later, after the interlocutor has quoted some lines from contemporary poetry, the satirist returns to physiological imagery [lines 103-6]: such bad poetry is emasculated stuff and its authors are eunuchs [103]; it is lame (delumbe, a metaphor from damaged hips); it is like saliva floating on the lips; it is wet. Yet Persius has not lost control of his imagery, for delumbe in line 104 echoes lumbum ("loins") in line 20, where the loins were the seat of sexual gratification, so that the attentive reader will be struck forcibly by the irony of the metaphor of impotence in lines 103-4. Again, the metaphor of the lips and saliva in 104-5 should be linked to the preliminary "gargle" of the dressed-up reciter in line 17 and the precious affectations of the equally gaudily dressed poet in 35, where it is the mouth that is the context of Persius's metaphors.

Persius's control is proved further by his return, immediately after lines 103-6, to his original metaphor of the ears [107-8], here "scraped" (_radere_: the metaphor is of a doctor cleaning an infected area of the skin) by the "biting truth" of the satirist. As we have seen, he makes a climax of his imagery of the ears by reference to the donkey's ears of King Midas [lines 119-21], answering the unfinished question of line 8. Finally, at line 126 he recalls the metaphor of cleansed ears, used earlier at line 107-8, in the "well-steamed" ear (_auris_, the nondiminutive form used now for the only time in this satire) of the listener capable of appreciating Persius's poetry.

At this stage the reader would be well advised to read through the first satire again. The complexity and apparent perversity of Persius's metaphorical writing will now be seen to be controlled by a certain logic, which rests upon a mastery of deliberate poetic techniques. One should remember also that the first satire is also an apologia, a program. Persius is contrasting his style with the smooth and effeminate stuff of his contemporaries: therefore the style of his poem is as essential as the meaning and the two cannot be separated. Its uncompromising idiosyncrasy is deliberate, the product of a master of poetic technique.

There are other occasions where a particular image gives direction to a whole passage. The last part of the third satire is built around the metaphor of disease [3.88-118], where the physical phenomena of disease are metaphors for the unseen passions of gluttony, avarice, lust, fear, and anger. Thus the union of the corporeal with the moral, of the concrete with the abstract, gives a vivid reality to the Stoic paradox "only the wise man is healthy." In the fifth satire images of the mouth direct the first twenty-nine lines: the _os modicum_ ("moderate mouth," line 15) of the satirist is contrasted with the hundred mouths of the bombastic epic and tragic poets [lines 1-4]; in lines 5-6 these mouths are stuffed with "robusti carminis offas" ("gobbets of strong verse"); at line 8 the eating of Procne's son and the banquet of Thyestes continue the metaphor of the mouth as a vehicle for something gross, so that the subjects of tragedy become metaphors for the grotesque horror of contemporary writing; at lines 10-13 the metaphor changes to the mouth blowing (that is, expelling air, as opposed to taking in food), with metaphors of bellows, of the hoarse cawing of a crow, and, finally, of children filling their cheeks and suddenly expelling the air with the sound that Persius imitates with the word scloppo [line 13]. Thus successive metaphors for the mouth introduce the satirist's announcement of his own disciplined style [lines 14-18]: once more the mythological banquet of Thyestes appears [lines 16-17], in contrast to the plebeia prandia ("common meals") of the satirist's conversational style. The mouth and its associated organs are finally used at 25-28, where "the tongue's painted surface" is contrasted with the vox pura ("genuine voice") of the sincere poet. The satirist concludes [26-29] that only in telling truthfully of his inmost feelings toward his teacher, could he call for the hundred mouths of the other poets.

Certain metaphors appear repeatedly. For example, since Persius adopts the persona of a literary and moral critic, metaphors for measurement and testing are important. At Satire 1.65-66 the metaphor of the carpenter's joint being tested for smoothness is used of the smooth style of contemporary poetry; it is followed by a simile of the artisan checking the straightness of a line with one eye closed. The metaphor of the carpenter correcting the straightness of a line with his rule (regula) is used with approbation at 5.38 of Cornutus straightening the morals of the young Persius. Here Persius neatly transfers to Latin poetry the Greek philosophical metaphor of the canon (that is, "ruler") as a measure of straightness. Again, at 4.10-13, the regula appears in a moral context, this time in an example where the philosophical student's judgment is correct even when the regula is itself out of the true (that is, as Casaubon explains, when the rule [regula] of justice needs to be tempered by equity). In this passage the regula is one of a series of measuring metaphors for ethical correctness: weighing in the scales [lines 10-11], the regula [lines 11-12], the condemnatory letter theta (line 13, for thanatos, the Greek word for death), used either by jurymen in written notes or placed in military lists before the names of soldiers killed in action.

Weighing in the scales becomes a metaphor for literary judgment at 1.6, and the same word (examen, "a
balance") is used at 5.101 for measuring out drugs. In
the latter passage the metaphor of the professional
apothecary is used for the properly trained philosopher
(21). At 5.47 the destinies of Cornutus and Persius
are equally balanced under the sign of Libra, while in
4.11-12 the political candidate knows how to weigh
justice in the scales, and how to tell if a right-angle
is true. At 3.82 professors are said to weigh words in
the scale, and at 1.86 the smooth defendant "balances"
the charges against him in "well-planed" antitheses:
here the metaphors of carpentry and weighing are
united.

Another repeated metaphor for testing is the potter's vessel. At 3.21-24 the immature and selfish
student is described as follows: "The jar sounds
cracked when struck; it does not ring true, with green
clay not properly fired. You are wet and soft clay,
and now, even now, you should hurry to be fashioned on
the turning wheel." Here Persius has expanded the Greek
metaphor, used by Plato, of testing the sound of the
potter's vessel, and has combined it with Horace's use
of the student as clay to be fashioned (22). He uses
the metaphor of testing the sound of a jar in a moral
context at 5.24-25, where, typically, he combines the
metaphor with two others--shaking out the folds of a
toga (excutienda, line 22) (23), and a painted stucco
surface ("pictae tectoria linguae" ["the covering of a
painted tongue," line 25]). As a result Persius is
able to expand his original metaphor (the jar) to refer
to literary as well as moral perfection. Finally, he
returns to the idea of the teacher as creator (in
conjunction with the metaphors of the carpenter's rule)
at 5.40, where Cornutus fashions the features of Persius's mind under his thumb--here a striking conjunction of the abstract mind with concrete features, the
thumb and the clay.

Finally, here are some random examples of single
metaphors that illuminate a particular passage and
raise it to a higher poetic level. Sometimes the
images are proverbial: at 4.23-24 people always look
at the knapsack (that is, of moral faults) on the back
of the person in front of them, never seeing their own.
This is a variation on the fable (told by Phaedrus,
4.10), in which Jupiter gives all human beings two

knapsacks, containing their own faults on their backs
and their neighbor's in front. There is a proverbial
air, too, about the metaphor at 5.92, where Persius
will "pluck the old grandmothers from your heart," that
is, remove the prejudices that his listener has learned
as a child from the old women in his family (24). Even
more striking is the fine metaphor at 5.70-72, where
the individual is the rear axle of a cart, never able
to catch up with the one in front. The image, which
may well be Persius's own invention, admirably compres-
ses the ideas of determinism in the individual's destiny, the onward progress of time never to be recaptured,
and the inexorable power of the turning wheels of
fortune. Other striking images are the dog dragging its
broken chain, for the man still partially enslaved to
his vices, at 5.159-60; the relay-race, for the heir
succeeding his predecessor, at 6.61; the roses blossom-
ing (in the old woman's prayer) wherever her child
walks, at 2.38; the rara avis ("rare bird") for an
impossibility, at 1.46 (25); the gambler's fingers,
gnarled like an old beech-tree at 5.59.

Meter and Diction

In order to convey a personal style of satire Persius needed to develop the satiric hexameter beyond
the conversational usage of Horace. The hexameter is
above all the meter of epic, and it was one of the
achievements of Lucilius that he adapted its noble
dignity to the less lofty style of satire. Horace
explains the difference between the two styles of hexameter in the fourth satire of his first book [lines 39-
62]. Discussing the conversational styles of Lucilius
and himself, he disclaims the title of "poetry" for
their verse, on the grounds that except for meter it
has nothing in common with the inspiration and grandeur
of true poetry. If, he concludes, you take away the
meter and jumble up the word-order, you would not have
poetry left, whereas lines of Ennius, however
butchered, would always show "disiecti membra poetae"
("the limbs of the dismembered poet"). Horace's dis-
claimer, of course, is part of his satiric persona, and
in fact he was a very polished versifier. But he
established the appropriately informal usage of the
hexameter for satire, and Persius in his prologue ac-

cepted the same principles, particularly that the satirist does not claim the inspiration of the Muses or the lofty dignity of the epic poet. Therefore he avoids epic diction and Vergilian rhythms except in passages where he is parodying epic. On the other hand, he goes beyond the Horatian practice in his greater use of dactylic rhythms and his avoidance of elision. It has been shown statistically that his hexameters are closer to the usage of Ovid than to that of Vergil and Horace (26). The only spondaic ending (that is --/-- in the fifth and sixth feet) is at 1.95, which comes in a passage of epic parody. Although he deplores the smooth style of his contemporaries, he avoids elision (which tends to interrupt the smooth flow of the hexameter), in the manner of Ovid, to a far greater extent than Horace. While he is more dactylic than Horace and Juvenal, he shows less metrical variety than both--for example fewer rhythmic patterns in any given passage, more repeated patterns and more lines in which word stress and metrical stress come together in the fourth foot. The difference from Horace can in part be accounted for by the enormous influence of Ovid, whose Metamorphoses (8 A.D.) appeared sixteen years after the death of Horace and nearly forty years after the completion of Horace's Satires, in part by the poetic conventions of the Neronian age. In sum, we can say that Persius developed a hexameter both vigorous and dignified, appropriate to the goals of his own satire yet in keeping with the conventions established by Horace. It achieves the strength and unity that Persius praised in Satire 1.92-106.

Like Horace Persius has a mastery of diction. He can parody epic; he can write dialogue or conversational sermo; he has passages of near-lyric beauty (for example, 1.39-40; 2.38; 5.41-44), which may, as in the case of the first two of these examples, be punctured immediately by a scornful return to the satiric mode. He offers passages of frank obscenity (for example, 1.87, 4.35-41, and 6.71-3) as well as passages of moral doctrine and literary criticism enlivened by gnomic or epigrammatic utterances (for example, the "one-liners" at 1.13, 1.6-7, 4.42, and 5.52). His comparative lack of metrical variety is amply compensated for by flexibility of style and by skilled and exact use of vocabulary and metaphor.

Irony and the Satirist's Persona

Persius's use of irony is neither so frequent nor so subtle as Horace's. In satire the essence of ironic technique is a persona that engages the listener yet gently deceives him, usually into siding unawares with the object of the satirist's attack, so that the satirist can say finally (as Horace did, Satire 1.1.69-70) "de te fabula narratur" ("You are the subject of my tale"). It is found most extensively in the sixth satire, where the satirist unexpectedly attacks frugality and supports the expenditure in moderation of one's goods on present pleasures. Since this is the most relaxed and urbane of the six satires, it is the most Horatian in tone. There is also a certain amount of irony in the third satire, where the satirist plays the part of the doctor and the listener cannot be too sure whether to identify with the satirist or with his patient. This is especially so in lines 107-18, where it is revealed that the listener, however objective he may claim to be, will have a hard time in denying that he too is liable to the passions criticized by the satirist.

In general, however, Persius's satiric persona is not as subtle and varied as that of Horace. On the other hand, it is a mistake to conclude from the persona that Persius was merely an immature young man of limited experience, gleaned mostly from books. The known facts of his life and his friendships disprove this facile estimate, as also does a critical reading of his poems. For the most part he comes on stage as a serious student of philosophy, certain of his Stoic principles, standing apart from the debased moral and literary criteria of his contemporaries, and speaking only to a select audience. He claims to attack without fear and appeals to the example of Lucilius in defense of his social criticism, while invoking also the less indirect methods of Horace [Satire 1.114-18]. For most of the first five satires his persona is fairly constant and generally predictable. What is surprising is the limited range of his Stoic doctrine. He lectures on fairly standard themes: prayer, avoidance of the passions, self-knowledge, true freedom achieved through correct moral philosophy. In the first satire, which in many ways is the most originial, he steps outside this narrow circle to deliver a brilliant critique of contemporary literary standards, and in the sixth he uses the persona of a genial friend to lead into the Epicurean disquisition on the proper use of one's wealth. Only in the first part of the fifth satire is the mask dropped to reveal the student and friend of Cornutus.

Conclusion

It remains to form a general assessment of Persius's style. He has generally been found obscure, and the great majority of critics have dismissed him as a poet who was too immature to be able to master poetic techniques. The metaphysical poet Abraham Cowley (himself one of the more obscure English poets) epitomizes this school of criticism: "Persius who you use to say, you do not know whether he be a good poet or no, because you cannot understand him, and who therefore [I say] I know to be not a good poet" (27).

Few would now adopt so simplistic an approach to poetry. Closer to the truth is Goethe's statement: "The author whom a lexicon can keep up with is worth nothing." We should allow, at least, that any poet worth the name makes intellectual demands upon the reader. There may be a concatenation of associations, images, symbols, or other indirect means of communication with the reader, and this fact is bound to lead to a measure of obscurity. In any case, the poet who deserves to be taken seriously is one who, first, is saying something worth communicating and, second, is in control of poetic techniques. As Ruskin put it: "The right of being obscure is not to be lightly claimed, it can only be founded on long effort to be intelligible." Unless one pedantically insists on the long effort (for Persius died young), Persius can justly claim this right. We have seen his precision in the choice words and images, and one need only read the first satire and the first part of the fifth to be assured that his obscurity is that of a master, not that of an immature apprentice.

A well-known passage from Ezra Pound's How to Read is helpful toward understanding the reasons for the difficulty of Persius (28). He attempts to define the ways in which language is "charged or energized," and

he distinguishes three "kinds of poetry":
Melopoeia, wherein the words are charged, over
and above their plain meaning, with some musical
property, which directs the bearing or trend of that
meaning.
Phanopoeia, which is the casting of images upon the
visual imagination.
Logopoeia, "the dance of the intellect among words,"
that is to say, it employs words not only for their
direct meaning, but it takes count in a special way
of habits of usage, of the context we expect to find
with the words, its usual concomitants, of its known
acceptances, and of ironical play. It holds the
aesthetic content which is peculiarly the domain of
verbal manifestation, and cannot possibly be contained in plastic or in music.

It is obvious that the latter two "kinds of poetry" are
especially relevant to the techniques of Persius, and
it is not surprising to find that he, more than any
other Latin poet, has suffered from the same uncompre-
hending criticism as many "obscure" modern poets. The
reason for this is in part explained by Pound in the
next passage after the one quoted above. "Phanopoeia,"
he says, "can . . . be translated almost . . . intact.
When it is good enough, it is practically impossible
for the translator to destroy it save by very crass
bungling. . . . Logopoeia does not translate; through
the attitude of mind it expresses may pass through a
paraphrase."
A poet who, like Persius, relies heavily on the
accurate use of words and metaphors is going to be at a
disadvantage with readers from other cultures and
languages than his own. Persius did not, admittedly,
help his own cause by his desire to appeal only to an
elite audience. Pound again has the appropriate
phrase, in discussing the French satirist Laforgue:
"he writes not the popular language of any country, but
an international tongue common to the excessively cultivated" (29).
Casaubon may have overstated the case for the
superiority of Persius's moral doctrines, but he was
closer to the truth than Dryden, who sneered that "his
verse is scabrous and hobbling, and his words not
everywhere well chosen" (30). In Dryden's view "the
purity of Latin" was more corrupted in Persius's time

than in that of Horace or even of Juvenal. Such criticism is circular: to set up a criterion of perfection (such as Augustan poetry) and then to shoot down those who wrote differently and in different times is to make a valid statement about taste but not a valid criticism of style. Dryden may be right to say (as he does) that Persius "cannot be allowed to stand in competition, either with Juvenal or Horace," an estimate that the vast majority of readers would agree with, but Persius's achievement in creating a unique style is undeniable. It is less gracious than the urbane satire of Horace, less powerful than the indignation of Juvenal. But at the very least it was a new stage in the development of Roman satire beyond Horace, and it prepared the way for Juvenal. Therefore Persius cannot be overlooked in the history of European satire, and his poetry justifiably asks of its readers the intellectual effort that any difficult literature requires. It is worth the effort to become one of the few for whom Persius was writing.

Chapter Seven
The Influence of Persius

Persius's book was edited and published by Cornutus and Caesius Bassus and was an immediate success: "Men immediately began to praise it and eagerly to get hold of it," says the Life. Before the end of the century it had become a classic. Quintilian ranked Persius as a satirist with Horace and said that his success was genuinely deserved, and the epigrammatist Martial contrasted the limited output of Persius with his great reputation (1). Unlike Juvenal, he does not seem to have suffered periods of eclipse in antiquity, nor does his style seem to have been attacked, as was that of him contemporary Lucan right from the first appearance of his epic. In part this is because Persius was less obviously rhetorical than Lucan, less superficially attractive than Seneca, whom, according to the Life, Persius did not find sympathetic. Above all, as Quintilian and Martial testify, the solid poetic qualities of Persius guaranteed his secure reputation.

Although satirists continued to write at Rome in the period after the death of Persius, the next major hexameter-satirist was Juvenal, whose first book of satires (nos. 1-5) was probably published about 105 A.D. Juvenal's indignation and rhetorical power have contributed to the eclipse of Persius in the last three centuries. His range of subjects is far wider (in Satire 1.85-86 he claims the whole of human activities and emotions as material for his satire), and he excels Persius in the variety of his persona and in brilliant sketches of life at Rome. Yet he could not have written as he did without the achievement of Persius, and it is wrong to attribute the foundations of Juvenal's satire only to Horace and Lucilius. In the first place, Persius brought the moral intensity of satire to a higher pitch, in part by concentrating upon a single subject for each satire, a unity not always achieved by the more discursive Horace. Juvenal followed Persius in this respect. Second, Persius's first satire set a new pattern for the program satire, which Juvenal

97

adopted in his first satire, one of his greatest.
Third, Juvenal was indebted to Persius's second satire
(on prayer) for his tenth, which has been the most
generally admired of his satires and was imitated by
Samuel Johnson in his Vanity of Human Wishes. Finally,
Persius's use of satire as a vehicle for moral doctrine affected the ethical side of Juvenal's poems.
Although Juvenal disclaims philosophical learning [Satire
13.120-25], it is an important quality in his satire,
as was recognized by Dryden and many others, but it has
often been underestimated because of the overwhelming
power of his rhetoric. Juvenal is the greater satirist, but in part he achieved greatness by emulating
Persius.

Persius was among the comparatively few pagan
authors whose moral doctrine appealed to the Christian
Fathers (2). He is quoted five times by Lactantius
(ca. 300 A.D.), four times for his doctrine of prayer
in satire 2. It is hardly surprising that passages
like the closing lines of the second satire (from which
Lactantius quotes twice) found favor with the Christian
Fathers, for their philosophy is as appropriate to
Christian as to pagan ethics.

At the other end of the fourth century Augustine and
Jerome both knew and quoted Persius. Augustine quoted
Persius ten times: for example, the gnomic lines of
Satire 3.66-72 on the human condition appealed espe-
cially to Augustine, who discovered in them a moral
loftiness that he found to be absent in pagan religion.
Again, he uses Persius's image of the painted stucco
[Satire 5.25] to illustrate by contrast the solidity of
Christian doctrine (3).

But it is Jerome who found Persius a most congenial
source of quotation and allusion for his own satirical
invective, especially in the Adversus Iovinianum. He
quotes Persius twenty times. Whereas other Christian
writers used Persius because of his moral doctrine,
Jerome, himself a formidable satirist, appreciated
Persius's satirical qualities. Thus he applies the
"fat beer-belly" of Satire 1.57 to Jovinianus and
likens him to the mad Orestes by quoting Satire 3.117-
18. He quotes the animal imitations of Satire 1.58-60,
and elsewhere he combines the colorful cornicari ("to
caw like a crow") of Satire 5.12 with the vivid image
of the professors weighing words in the scale from
Satire 3.82 (4). It is clear that Jerome understood

the style, as opposed to the doctrine, of Persius far more perceptively than other Christian writers. About the time that Augustine and Jerome were writing, in 402 A.D., an imperial official called Flavius Julius Tryfonianus Sabinus was reading Persius at Barcelona and Toulouse. At the end of his copy he wrote that he had tried to correct the text without a master copy, a vivid glimpse of the life of educated Romans even as the empire was disintegrating. Sabinus's copy is lost, but two manuscripts, descended from it and written respectively in the ninth and tenth centuries, still survive and are among the principal sources for the text of Persius.

Throughout late antiquity and the early Middle Ages Persius continued to be read and quoted. He was a quarry for grammarians and commentators: for example, the polymath bishop of Seville, Isidore (ca. 625), quotes him nine times in his Origines. The obscurity of Persius does not seem to have been a handicap for his readers even in an age of declining scholarship, and his moral doctrines ensured his continued survival after the triumph of Christianity. He was read by scholars in every part of Europe. The monks of Britain were familiar with him, and he is quoted by the historian Bede and the great educator and writer Alcuin of York. Alcuin was the most important intellectual figure in the eighth-century renaissance of learning under Charlemagne, and Persius is quoted (although not extensively) by many Carolingian writers, including Paul the Deacon and Theodulf. More important to the transmission of Persius was the fact that his poems were copied in the Benedictine monasteries under the Carolingians. The principal manuscript upon which the modern text is based was written at the monastery of Lorsch in the ninth century (5), and the two manuscripts mentioned above as descended from Sabinus's copy are both Carolingian. Besides these three, there are many other manuscripts surviving from before 1000 A.D., and the total number of extant manuscripts has been estimated at over 150. There could hardly be better proof of the continued interest in Persius throughout the Middle Ages.

During these centuries Persius continued to be quoted, and he appears in authors as widely apart in time and place as Remigius (ninth century), Gerbert (tenth century: he later became Pope Silvester

II), and Peter Abelard (twelfth century), in France;
William of Malmesbury and John of Salisbury in
twelfth century England (John especially used Persius,
quoting him more than twenty times); in Italy he appears
in the works of Bishop Rather of Verona (tenth century)
and of the tenth century historian Liutprand, bishop of
Cremona. Finally, he was widely read and quoted by a
host of medieval writers in Germany. The opening words
of Persius's first satire, "O curas hominum," are
quoted at the beginning of a satire on the vanity of
court life in the collection of medieval poems known as
the Carmina Burana (6). And in Italy, at the threshold
of the Renaissance, Dante placed Persius with Vergil
and Homer in the first circle of Hell among the select
group of the best and most moral pagan writers (7). In
general, however, the principle held true that Persius
was popular because of his moral, rather than poetic or
satiric, qualities, and Jerome remained the conspicuous
exception among the many who quoted him.
     With the coming of printing the widespread publica-
tion of Persius, that had led to the copying of so many
medieval manuscripts, continued. The first printed
texts appeared in Rome (1469-70) and Venice (1470) and
are among the earliest printed books. Within the next
few years texts were printed in France (Paris, 1472),
Switzerland (Basel, 1474), and Germany (Leipzig, 1492),
as well as in Italy. The earliest edition with commentary was that by Bartolomeo Fonte, published in Venice
in 1480. It is interesting that Fonte, in his prefa-
tory address to Lorenzo di Medici, rates Persius above
all other poets for his moral qualities and finds his
style (including vocabulary and juxtaposition of
figures of speech) exceptional. Since Fonte the flood
of editions has never slackened. No less than 378
editions were published in Europe before 1800, and more
than 100 have been published or reissued since then.
The first American edition was by F. P. Leverett,
headmaster of the Boston Latin School, and was published at Boston in 1832; it was often reprinted, until it
was replaced by the edition of Basil Gildersleeve (New
York, 1875) (8).
     The most important edition of Persius was published
at Paris in 1605 by Isaac Casaubon. Casaubon was in
part responding to the ferocious criticism of Persius
by the great classical scholar J. C. Scaliger, whose
Poetics was published at Lyons in 1561. The debate is

worth detailed attention, as the opposing positions with regard to Persius have not changed since the sixteenth century. Scaliger rated Persius far below Juvenal and Horace, characterizing the three satirists as follows: "Juvenal is fiery; he attacks openly and cuts your throat; Persius is arrogant (Persius insultat): Horace smiles." Further, he found the style of Persius "morose" and "lacking in wit, for, while he wished his writing to be read, he did not want it to be understood." Finally, Persius liked to parade his "fevered learning": he was both obscure and obscene (9).

Scaliger's criticisms have been echoed by countless commentators down to the present time, and like many damaging literary attacks they are partly true. They are widest of the mark in their underestimate of Persius's style and of the moral qualities of his satire. In reply Casaubon defended Persius for his superiority in moral doctrine, which, with wit, he identified as the essential quality of good satire. The quality of Persius's wit is a matter of subjective judgment, but its existence cannot be denied. As for moral doctrine, Casaubon was following the judgment of Persius's readers over 1,500 years, and few would quarrel with it. Casaubon, indeed, overstated the case for Persius and was harshly criticized for this by Dryden, who nevertheless agreed that Persius's moral doctrine and philosophical consistency were superior to those of Horace and equal to those of Juvenal (10).

Despite his partisan arguments, Casaubon's edition of Persius is one of the great monuments of classical scholarship. Indeed, the younger Scaliger sarcastically commented: "with Casaubon's Persius the sauce is better than the fish." Casaubon's Prolegomena contain a brilliant analysis of the nature of satire, and the commentary has never been equaled for its discernment and breadth of learning. All commentators since Casaubon have been in his debt, as a glance at any modern commentary will show. After Casaubon, Persius was taken seriously as a poet as well as a moralist. The great majority of readers have sided with Scaliger and Dryden in being discouraged by his obscurity, but all who have made the effort to read him with understanding have recognized both the moral and poetic qualities that have deservedly made him one of the greatest satirists.

The seventeenth century was the high-water mark of
Persius's fortunes since the Renaissance. Throughout
Europe he was read and quoted: here we will focus only
upon his importance in France and England.

The taste for Latin satire in France had been established early in the seventeenth century by Mathurin
Régnier (1573-1613), who adapted the three major Latin
satirists extensively (11). Boileau (1636-1711), associated himself with Régnier specifically as a follower
of Persius and Horace: "studieux amateur et de Perse
et d'Horace,/assez près de Régnier m' asseoir sur le
Parnasse . . ." ("a studious lover both of Persius and
of Horace, to be seated near Régnier on Parnassus,"
Epistle 10.101-02); but his use of Persius extends far
further than that of Régnier (12). His debt to Horace
is, to be sure, more pervasive, and he adapts or imitates whole satires of Juvenal (most notably Juvenal's
third and sixth in his sixth and tenth respectively),
but he seems to have had a special sympathy for
Persius. Like Persius he wrote satire young (by the
age of twenty-eight, Persius's age at his death,
Boileau had composed seven of his twelve satires), and,
as with Persius, his independent financial means gave
his satire an added dimension of freedom, to which he
refers in his Discours sur la Satire of 1668, invoking
the example of Persius. He shared with Persius the
view that literary and moral criticism are often one
and the same. His moral doctrine is consistent with
Stoicism, despite (or perhaps because of) his devout
Catholicism, for he was sympathetic to the austere
doctrines of the Jansenists. Like Persius, also, he
does not state new or even profound moral truths, while
he shares with Persius the capacity for transforming
moral commonplaces into lofty poetry. His style is
less complex than that of Persius, his metaphors less
strained. His satire, like that of Persius and far
more than that of Horace, indulges in direct attacks on
contemporary authors. In keeping with the taste of the
age he eschews the physical coarseness that is so
obvious a feature of Persius's style.

Boileau elegantly summarizes the essential qualities
of Persius: "Perse, en ses vers obscurs, mais serrés
et pressants,/Affecta d'enfermer moins de mots que de
sens" ("Persius, in his lines obscure but closely woven
and urgent, managed to include more sense than words,"
Art Poétique 2.155-56). In his adaptations of Persius,

however, he makes greater use of the content of his satires than the style, whose intensity and complexity he understood so well. A few selections must suffice from many imitations and allusions. His most explicit defense of satire is the ninth satire, and it has much in common with the two program-satires of Persius and Juvenal. For example, in lines 243-66 Boileau distinguishes between his virile satire and the affected effusions of his feeble contemporaries (dismissed as "sugary" with a "spirit of dulled softness," words that echo Persius's scornful *tener* and *mollis*, "tender" and "soft"). He imitates Persius's claim to speak freely [Persius, *Satires* 1.107-34], in several places, for example, in *Satires* 1.145-56 and 7.73-93. He quotes Persius's use of King Midas's ears [Persius, 1.119-21] at *Satire* 9.220-24, and the end of *Epistle* 9 [lines 169-74] expands the idea at the end of Persius's first satire [*Satire* 1.134]. The most extended adaptation of Persius is in Boileau's eighth satire, lines 65-89, where the tyranny of avarice is closely modeled on Persius's vigorous personification in *Satire* 5.132-60. Again, the passage on the conquest of the passions, which Boileau sets in Christian terms in *Epistle* 9.91-98, is similar to the Stoic doctrine of Persius, for example in *Satire* 3.109-11.

Boileau's influence on satire, indeed on poetic taste, in general, in France and England is so extensive that his use of Persius is in itself important in the history of classical literary influences. No other major satirist appreciated Persius so deeply, and it is largely through him that the moral and literary standards of Persius became part of the canon of taste well into the eighteenth century.

Meanwhile, the satiric tradition had developed somewhat differently in England. Sir Thomas Wyatt (1502-42) imitated Horace and Juvenal in his three satires, but has few traces of Persius. The style of John Donne (1573-1631), however, is like that of Persius in its complexity, and in his *Satires* and *Elegies* he can be as obscure as in his metaphysical *Songs and Sonnets*. It is easy to recognize Donne's adaptations of Horace (for example, his fourth satire imitates the ninth satire of Horace's first book), but it is in his persona and style that he is closer to Persius. In the very first lines of his first satire he adopts the independent, serious persona of Persius:

Away thou fondling motley humorist,
Leave me, and in this standing wooden chest
Consorted with these few books, let me lie
In prison, and here be coffined, when I die. . . .

There is an echo of Persius's words scribimus inclusi
("we write, shut in" Satire 1.13), and a general sympathy with his attitude. In his fifth satire Donne
climaxes a series of images for greedy courtiers with
one that is worthy of Persius's coarseness: "officers/
are the devouring stomach, and suitors/ the excrements,
which they void" [Satire 5.17-19]. A few lines later
his metaphor and moral tone recall Persius: [I] now
begin/To know and weed out this enormous sin./O age of
rusty iron!" [Satire 5.33-35].

It was with Dryden, however, that the debate between
Scaliger and Casaubon was settled, for he assured the
victory among English satirists of Horatian urbanity as
against the complexity of Persius. Dryden prefaced his
translation of Persius and Juvenal (1693) with the
Discourse concerning the Original and Progress of Satire,
to which reference has been made above. As one who had
diligently translated Persius, he spoke with the authority of experience, and his characterization of Persius's verse as "scabrous and hobbling" permanently
damaged Persius's reputation. (That he found Horace's
style "generally grovelling" seems to have been overlooked.) He carefully weighs the merits of Horace,
Persius, and Juvenal and answers the arguments of
Casaubon. Not surprisingly for the author of Absalom
and Achitophel and MacFlecknoe, he follows Scaliger by
giving Juvenal the prize, Horace the second place, and
Persius the last. His judgment has been more or less
the accepted opinion since then, except in periods (for
example the mid-eighteenth century) when the urbanity
of Horace has been preferred to the indignation of
Juvenal. Yet the positive side of Dryden's examination
should not be forgotten. While he deplored the
obscurity of Persius, he also appreciated his consistency, sincerity, and moral seriousness. In these
respects, he concludes, Persius "excels Horace . . .
and is equal to Juvenal, who was as honest and serious
as Persius, and more he could not be." Finally, it
should be remembered that Dryden found all three
"Ancients" preferable to "the Moderns" and he granted
Persius "victory not only over all the Grecians, who

were ignorant of the Roman satire, but over all the
Moderns in succeeding ages; excepting Boileau and your
Lordship" (13).
Since Dryden's time Persius has been more or less in
eclipse. He has, as he would have wished, been read by
the discriminating few, but his influence has been
minimal in comparison to that of Horace and Juvenal.
Pope (1688-1744), the greatest of English satirists, is
also the most Horatian, except in passages of Juvena-
lian invective. He has few direct reminiscences of
Persius. In the Epistle to Dr. Arbuthnot, which is the
equivalent of a program-satire, he adapts the form and
content of the discussion of the satirist's freedom in
the last part of Persius's first satire. In particular, he uses the legend of Midas's ears and expands
Persius, lines 119-21:

P.   'Tis sung, when Midas' ears began to spring
       (Midas a sacred person and a king)
       His very minister who spied them first
       (Some say his queen) was forced to speak or
         burst:
       And is not mine, my friend, a sorer case,
       When every coxcomb perks them in my face?
A.   Good friend, forbear! You deal in dangerous
        things,
       I'd never name queens, ministers or kings:
       Keep close to ears, and those let asses prick,
       'Tis nothing--P. Nothing? If they bite and
        kick?
       Out with it, Dunciad! let the secret pass,
       That secret to each fool, that he's an ass:
       The truth once told (and wherefore should we
        lie?)
       The Queen of Midas slept, and so may I. (14)

In his Imitation of The Sixth Epistle of the First Book
of Horace Pope was clearly imitating Persius on Avarice
[Satire 5.132] with line 112, "Up, up! cries Gluttony,
'tis the break of day," where Horace [Epistle 1.6.56-
61] had no such personification. It is in his letters
that Pope lets us know what he thinks of Persius (15).
Twice he quotes Persius, Satire 5.41-44, with approval,
and prefers those lines to Dryden's choices, which were
the closing lines [73-75] of the second satire (much
admired, as we have seen, in late antiquity and the

Middle Ages) and the shipwreck in Satire 6.27-31. Dryden maintained that except for these lines "our Poet has written nothing Elegantly" (16). Pope, rather, admired the lines on friendship that Persius addressed to Cornutus [5.41-44]: "How beautiful are those lines of Persius, and there are not many so, though there are many very sensible and philosophical." He also admired Persius for his outspokenness under the tyranny of Nero, which, as we have seen, he imitated in The Epistle to Dr. Arbuthnot.

No other English poet of the first rank since Pope has been obviously influenced by Persius. The minor satirist William Gifford (1756-1826) published The Baviad in 1791. It is quite a lively imitation of Persius's first satire, but its esoteric subject (literary squabbles of the day) and its length (three times that of Persius's first satire) have rightly relegated it to the curiosities of English literature. Other imitations of less merit have been published-- Advice to an Aspiring Young Gentleman of Fortune in Imitation of the Fourth Satyr of Perseus [sic] was offered for "Price six-pence" in London in 1733, and the curious Persius Redivivus: A Satire, by "An Eton Boy" (published at Eton in 1832), shows that at least Persius maintained a place in the Latin Curriculum. In the United States Persius was apparently still regularly studied late in the nineteenth century, since B. L. Gildersleeve, according to his preface, undertook his edition in 1875 in part to make Persius "less distasteful to the general student." Persius did not figure in Thomas Jefferson's catalog for a gentleman's library, in response to Robert Skipwith's request for "books . . . suited to the capacity of a common reader who understands but little of the classicks and who has not leisure for any intricate or tedious study" (17).

It is a curious fact that while so few readers have been prepared to give time and effort to Persius's Latin, there have been a large number of translations into English, German, French, and Italian (18). There are no less than fourteen published translations into English verse, including two within the last twenty years. In addition there have been at least six English prose translations. The heroic couplets of Dryden (1693) have been the most influential in setting the criteria of literary taste through which English readers have become familiar with Persius, and for 125 years these criteria were dominant. At least this style retains much of the dignity and wit of the Latin original, but Persius loses more in translation than most authors, because of the complexity of his metaphorical writing and his accuracy in choice of words. In addition, heroic couplets have a regularity and balance that are too monumental for the angular asymmetry of Persius. Finally, his obscenity is an insuperable stumbling-block, as Dryden admitted. Solutions to the problem have varied with the conventions of the day. Dryden in the fourth satire substituted an equally coarse diatribe for that of Persius, while Drummond (1797), faced with lines 33-41 of the fourth satire, composed thirty lines of paraphrase, as he said, "rather founded upon Persius, than imitated from him." Other translators have simply omitted the offensive passages. In our own time, however, the clinical frankness of Merwin (1961) is too strong for the subtle techniques of Persius.

Persius is unlikely to recover the high standing that he enjoyed before the eighteenth century. His style is too difficult and his range too limited for the judgment of Dryden ever to be reversed. Yet he is in the front rank of satirists and the significance of his satires to the history of satire is out of all proportion to their bulk. Above all, he is a poet whose complexities cannot obscure, and often enhance, poetic truths that are universally applicable.

Notes and References

Chapter One

1. Cato the Younger, also known as Cato Uticensis, had been the leader of the opposition to Julius Caesar. After Caesar's victory at Thapsus (in Africa) in 46 B.C. Cato retreated to Utica, where he committed suicide rather than submit to Caesar. He became the great example of the person who would rather die than give up liberty, and he was especially revered by Stoics. His nephew, Brutus, was Caesar's murderer (44 B.C.), in part inspired by his uncle's principles. Persius refers to Cato's dying words, which had become a standard passage to be learned by heart, at _Satire_ 3.44–47.

2. Conington's note on _Satire_ 2.14.

3. See M. Morford, "The Neronian Literary Revolution," _C. J._ 68 (1973):210–15. A reliable survey of Nero's reign is B. H. Warmington, _Nero: Reality and Legend_ (London, 1969). The massive study of E. Cizek, _L'Époque de Néron et ses Controverses Ideologiques_ (Leiden: Brill, 1971), has much information on the cultural aspects of Nero's reign but is unreliable and generally disappointing.

4. The best account of the Golden House is by J. B. Ward-Perkins, "The Golden House of Nero," _Antiquity_ 30 (1956):209–19. The primary sources are Tacitus, _Annals_ 15.42 and Suetonius, _Nero_, 31. For the development of the literary tradition about the Golden House, see M. Morford, "The Distortion of the Domus Aurea Tradition," _Eranos_ 56 (1968):158–79.

5. The conspiracy is described by Tacitus, _Annals_ 15.48–74.

6. Suetonius describes Nero's death, _Nero_, 49.

7. There are good general accounts of Stoicism by F. H. Sandbach, _The Stoics_ (London: Chatto and Windus, 1975), and by J. M. Rist, _Stoic Philosophy_ (Cambridge: Cambridge University Press, 1969). E. V. Arnold, _Roman Stoicism_ (London: Routledge and Kegan Paul, 1909), is

still useful although dated. The Stoic fragments are
assembled in J. von Arnim, Stoicorum Veterum Fragmenta
(Leipzig: Teubner, 1921-24).
8. Tacitus, Annals 16.22.

Chapter Two

1. Quintilian, 10.1.93: "satura quidem tota
nostra est" ("Satire indeed is entirely Roman").
2. An excellent and balanced survey of the problems is in the second chapter of Michael Coffey,
Roman Satire (London, 1976).
3. See ibid., chap. 8-10.
4. See ibid., chap. 4, for Lucilius. The brief
remarks by Rudd, with quotations from Lucilius, in the
introduction to his translation of Horace and Persius,
pp. 3-7, are instructive. The fragments of Lucilius
are conveniently collected and translated by E. H.
Warmington, Remains of Old Latin, vol. 3 (London:
Heinemann, 1938). References to fragments of Lucilius
and other early Latin authors from Warmington's edition
are given by the number followed by "W" (for example,
"fr. 632 W").
5. See Coffey, Roman Satire, 92-93, for a brief
account of Hellenistic influences on Horatian satire.
6. For the Cynics see D. R. Dudley, A History of
Cynicism (London: Methuen, 1937).
7. Diogenes Laertius, 4.46-58; Horace, Satire
2.2.60. For the Hellenistic dialogue the standard work
is R. Hirzel, Der Dialog (Leipzig: Teubner, 1895).
8. An excellent study of the iambic tradition and
its influence on Roman satire is by M. Puelma Piwonka,
Lucilius und Kallimachos (Frankfurt, 1949); pp. 358-67
are especially useful for Persius.
9. G. A. Gerhard, Phoinix von Kolophon (Leipzig:
Teubner, 1909), is a mine of information on Hellenistic
iambics and epigrams: pp. 228-84 are especially useful
for gnomic epigrams. The fragments of Hipponax and
Phoenix are collected and translated by A. D. Knox in
Herodes, Cercidas and The Greek Choliambic Poets
(London: Heinemann, 1929)--(Loeb Classical Library:
bound with Theophrastus, Characters). The standard
text is E. Diehl, Anthologia Lyrica Graeca (Leipzig:
Teubner, 1936), vol. 1, pt. 3.
10. Lucilius, fr. 957-60 W.
11. For a representative select

introduction, pp. 4-6 (see note 4 above).
  12. Lucilius, fr. 1000-1001 W; Horace, Satire 2.1.85;
Persius Satire 1.109-10.
  13. Lucilius, fr. 844 W; 401-10 W.
  14. For Horace's satires see Coffey, Roman Satire,
chap. 5. The best study of the satires is N. Rudd,
The Satires of Horace (Cambridge, 1966). Coffey, pp.
226-27, has a manageable selection of other references
from the vast bibliography on Horace.
  15. Lucilius, fr. 1063; 1066-74; 1077-83; 1085-89 W.
See also the witty anecdote at fr. 87-93 W.
  16. Dante, Inferno 4.88-90. The other three poets
were Homer, Ovid, and Lucan.

Chapter Three

  1. The basic article on the prologue is by J. H.
Waszink, "Das Einleitungsgedicht des Persius," Wiener
Studien 76 (1963):79-91. From the large number of
other discussions the relevant pages in Reckford's
article in Hermes 90 (1962):501-3, are to be recom-
mended. Scivoletto prints the choliambics at the end
of his text and denies that they are a prologue.
  2. Ennius's dream is fr. 4-14 W in Warmington's
Remains of Old Latin, vol.1 (London: Heinemann, 1956).
Persius refers to it again at Satire 6.10-11.
  3. Caballus (with its related adjective
caballinus) is a vulgar word for "horse" instead of the
more noble equus: an English approximation would be
"nag" or "gee-gee." Labra prolui ("I wet my lips") is
also a deflationary phrase for drinking at the Fountain
of the Muses. The French satirist, Régnier (ca. 1600),
similarly treated Pegasus in an undignified way in
lines 43-44 of his ninth satire, referring to bad
critics: "il semble, en leurs discours hautains et
généreux,/que le cheval volant n'ait pissé que pour
eux" ("it seems, in their lofty and high flown disqui-
sitions, that the flying horse pissed only for them").
  4. Athenaeus, 8.59.359e. Songs sung by Greek
children dressed as birds are discussed by A. Dieterich
in Kleine Schriften (Leipzig: Teubner, 1911), pp. 337-
44. The magpie in Petronius is at Satyricon 28. The
Latin version of Aesop's fable of the crow is Phaedrus
1.13. Callimachus, Iamb. 2 (=9.162 Pf.) may have influenced Persius. For rejection of the Muses by Lucilius and Persius see Puelma Piwonka, Lucilius, pp. 358-64.

5. Line 12: Persius's _cachinno_ (to be taken as a verb, "I laugh loudly") alludes both to Horace's _ridentem dicere verum_: "to tell the truth with a laugh" (_Satire_ 1.1.24), discussed above in chap. 2, p. 30, and to the Greek concept of _to spoudogeloion_ ("serious laughing"). He may also have had Democritus (ca. 420 B.C.) in mind, who was known as the "laughing philosopher," described by Juvenal in _Satire_ 10.33-35.

6. For the literary and other overtones in these lines see Bramble, 75-77. _Plasma, patrare, fractus,_ and _ocellus_ all have moral or sexual connotations, while the first two also appear in literary criticism. Quintilian 1.8.2 and 11.3.76 show clearly how Persius succeeds in combining the vocabularies of literary and moral criticism.

7. The difficulties of lines 19-23 are insuperable. They are discussed at length by J. C. Bramble, _Persius and the Programmatic Satire_ (Cambridge, 1974), pp. 78-90, 146-48, whose interpretation of lines 22-23 is untenable. I have translated Madvig's emendation _articulis_ in 23 for the MS _auriculis_, and have preferred Casaubon's interpretation of _cute perditus_, as a reference to dropsy, to Bramble's explanation of it in sexual terms. Horace, _Satire_ 2.5.96-98, is the obvious source for Persius's imagery. In Horace the flatterer "blows up the swelling bladder" until his victim cries out "Enough!" (_ohe!_). A further difficulty is the imagery of "collecting titbits for others' ears," where the ears are the way by which other senses than hearing receive gratification. The imagery of Satire 1 is well discussed by Coffey, _Roman Satire_, pp. 113-14, with references on p. 240.

8. The lines were said by the scholiast (an ancient commentator who annotated a manuscript) to be Nero's. Despite the authority of Casaubon, who agreed with the scholiast, there is no proof of Nero's authorship, while the objections to this view are overwhelming. Persius is attacking the literary taste of the age, not the poetic effusions of the emperor.

9. This must be the reference in lines 108-9: _limina_ is the entrance to the patron's house where the client waits to be admitted, rather than the place where the patron's dog snarls. The snarling dog is the satirist, and _hic_ in line 109 refers to his satire.

10. Lines 112-14 parody warning inscriptions and notices. That statues were targets for such attentions

may be inferred also from Horace, Satire 1.8.38-39 and Juvenal, Satire 1.131. Here the satirist describes himself appropriately as one who defiles with his criticism the pure but specious facade of Roman society.

11. The story is told by Ovid, Met. 11.180-83. The barber dug a hole into which he whispered "King Midas has ass's ears," and reeds sprung up which repeated the secret to the world at large. The story in the Life (lines 55-59 in the O.C.T.) and in the scholiast on line 121--that a reference to Nero stood originally in this line--is without foundation.

12. Line 134: "in the morning I give them the edict and after lunch Callirhoe." The edict is some public announcement (Rudd translates as "Law reports"), and Callirhoe must be the title of a trashy play or mime on a par with the literary productions criticized by Persius and therefore suitable for the common crowd.

Chapter Four

1. There is a reference here to a well-known passage in Horace, Satire 2.6.10-13.

2. Memorabilia 1.3.3; cf. Plato, Euthyphro 14e. Persius keeps the idea of bargaining in the repeated use of emere ("to buy") and its derivatives and in the word merces ("payment") in line 29.

3. The punctuation and division between the speakers follows the interpretation of A. E. Housman in C.Q. 7 (1913):16-18, which is accepted by Clausen in the O.C.T. text. A different but acceptable arrangement is followed by Rudd in his translation and is explained by him in C.R. 20 (1970):286-88.

4. An idea also familiar from the famous "choice of Hercules," who chose the hard upward road to Virtue as against the broad and easy way of Vice. Hence Hercules was one of the mythological figures used by the Stoics as an ideal example.

5. Horace Satire 1.3.123-42) had ridiculed the Stoic philosopher at the end of his third satire, using the paradox "only the philosophers are kings" as the occasion of boys' taunts.

6. This was the view of Casaubon and Dryden and is still accepted by Bo. Dryden further believed that Socrates in Persius stood for Seneca.

7. Valerius Maximus, 3.1.ext.1.

8. Dessen has useful discussions of the rela-

tionshp of the fourth satire to the First Alcibiades
(pp. 58-70) and of the Sokratikoi logoi (pp. 97-105).
    9. Aesop, fable 359, reproduced by Phaedrus, 4.10.
It is referred to by Catullus (22.21) and Horace
(Satire 2.3.299), and appears in Seneca's De Ira,
3.28.8.
    10. Lines 47-49; cf. Satire 3.109-18, where the
examples are more extended and less obscure. In 4.48
the unexpected use of penem for mentem ("if you do
whatever occurs to your penis" for "your mind") is a
noteworthy example of Persius's technique. It makes
the point forcefully that it is the passions, not the
mind, that rule the young man's life. Line 49, which
appears to refer to usury, has never been satisfactor-
ily explained.

Chapter Five

    1. Cicero, Paradox.Stoic.34: "quid est libertas?
potestas vivendi ut velis" ("What is liberty? The
power of living as you wish").
    2. Lines 1-2. Homer, first in the field, had more
modestly called for ten (Iliad 2.489). In first century B.C. the epic poet Hostius increased this to 100
(F.P.L. 33, fr. 3), as did Vergil in the Georgics
(2.43) and Aeneid (6.625).
    3. The Muse is given her Roman title, Camena, in
line 21. The Greek Muses were dismissed in line 7.
    4. Bramble's introductory chapter (Persius, pp. 1-
15) on "Style and expression in Persius's fifth satire"
is a perceptive commentary on lines 14-16 and 19-29.
The reader will find there references to the relevant
scholarship for which the present work does not have
room. Bramble's conclusion is wrong: "We are sometimes given the impression that Persius was writing
specimens of satire, rather than satire itself." In
any case these words appear to contradict Bramble's own
analysis of Persius's apologia.
    5. The closest parallels are Horace's tributes to
his father (Satire 1.6.65-99) and to Maecenas (Satire
1.6.1-6 and 45-64).
    6. This is explained by the Augustan poet
Manilius, whose long poem Astronomicon dealt with
astrology: see 2.616-19. The baleful influence of
Saturn is referred to by Horace, Carmina 2.17.22-25, in
a passage that Persius is certainly imitating.

7. Temperare has the basic sense of moderating and adjusting. When used of adjusting two separate entities to each other, it appears to have the sense of mixing in the proper proportion. Thus it expresses the sense of Greek words connected with harmony. Horace, Epistle 2.2.187, uses it in this sense of a man's Genius (that is, guardian spirit) "tempering" one's birth-constellation, a passage that Persius is probably imitating. Temperare is closer to the Greek concepts of adjusting and fitting than is the more passive consentire ("to feel together," "to agree"), that is used in line 46.

8. Dama, short for Demetrius, was frequently used by Horace for a slave's name: for example Satires 1.6.38; 2.5.18 and 101; 2.7.54.

9. Menander's play (of which only fragments are extant) was adapted by the Latin comic poet, Terence (ca. 165 B.C.). This scene was also used by Horace in Satire 2.3.259-71.

10. Persius had used the "hairy centurion" for the same purpose at Satire 3.77.

11. D. Henss, "Die Imitationstechnik des Persius," Philologus 99 (1955):277-94: reprinted in D. Korzeniewski, ed., Die römische Satire (Darmstadt, 1970), pp. 365-83.

12. Horace's views are perhaps best expressed in the beautiful ode to Dellius, Carmina 2.3, or in that to Licinius, 2.10, in which [line 5] the Golden Mean is named.

13. The act of harmonious composition is expressed by the Latin word intendisse (lit. "to have stretched tight"), the technical term for tuning a stringed instrument. The whole passage, lines 3-4, is full of difficulty and ambiguity. It is exhaustively discussed by H. Beikircher, Kommentar zur VI. Satire des A. Persius Flaccus, Wiener Studien, supp. 1 (Vienna, 1969), pp. 22-24.

14. Perhaps the quotation is from the Satires, as attributed by O. Skutsch, Studia Enniana (London: Athlone Press, 1968, pp. 25-29. It is certainly not from the Annales, to which Warmington assigns it, R.O.L., vol. 1, fr. 14 W. Ennius in the prologue to the Annales had described how the soul of Homer had transmigrated to him, having previously been a peacock. Transmigration of souls was a Pythagorean doctrine, hence Persius's expression [9-10] "after Quintus (Ennius) had stopped

snoring (dreaming of) being Homer via a Pythagorean
peacock." Another reference to Ennius's dream is in
Persius's choliambic prologue, line 2.
     15. Horace, Epistle 2.2.190-94.
     16. Bestius is an Horatian figure from Epistle
1.15.27. His attitude in Persius 6.37-40 is like that
of the "hairy centurions" in Satire 3.77-87, and the
"varicose centurion" Pulfenius in 5.189-91.
     17. The German "victory" of Caligula is related
by Suetonius, Gaius 43, and Tacitus, Germania 37.
Persius enjoys the details, for example, the hired
"prisoners" and the wigs for the "Germans" in the
triumphal procession.
     18. Lines 51-52 cannot be satisfactorily
explained. In the text the meaning is taken as "[I
will not tell you what I think because] the field
nearby still has a lot of stones in it [for people to
throw at me]." But there is much to be said for the
view that the heir's words in line 51, non adeo, mean
"I do not accept the inheritance (because you have
frittered it all away)," taking adeo as a verb rather
than adverb. See N. Rudd's helpful note in The Satires
of Horace and Persius (Harmondsworth, 1973), p. 184.
Beikircher, Kommemtar zur VI Satire, pp. 90-97, is
exhaustive, and the notes to lines 51-52 of D. Bo, A.
Persii Flacci Saturarum Liber (Turin, 1960) and R. A.
Harvey, A Commentary on Persius (Leiden, 1981) set out
the alternatives.
     19. Chrysippus was head of the Stoic school of
Athens in the later part of the third century B.C. The
problem of his heap (Latin acervus, Greek sorites) was
as follows: at what point does a collection of
individual items become a finite entity? Is one orange
a heap, or three, or ten? If you say, for example,
"ten is a heap," then if you take one away is nine not
a heap? The logical problem is apparently insoluble,
as Seneca said in discussing good deeds (De Beneficiis,
5.19.9): "So when does good exist as an entity? For
the well-known sorites is applicable, which cannot be
given a defined limit, because it increases little by
little and continues to creep ahead." Paradoxes and
riddles were a favorite method of argument with the
Stoics: technically the sorites was an adynaton
("impossibility"). Cicero, Academica 2.93, has an
anecdote of Chrysippus's use of the
sorites.

Chapter Six

1. John Dryden, A Discourse concerning the Original and Progress of Satire (1693) in John Dryden: Selected Criticism, ed. J. Kinsley and G. Parfitt (Oxford: Oxford University Press, 1970), p. 247. References in this chapter and chapter 7 are taken from this work. The Discourse is on pp. 208-78: pp. 245-53 and 261-62 for Persius. The magisterial and persuasive prose of Dryden should be tempered, however, by a critical approach; see the excellent remarks of N. Rudd. The Satires of Horace (Cambridge: Cambridge University Press, 1966), pp. 258-73.

2. In "Studies in Persius," Hermes 90 (1962):483.

3. Horace, Carmina. 3.1.37-40.

4. J. P. Sullivan, "In defence of Persius," Ramus 1 (1972):48-62; see p. 57 for quotation.

5. Of the 701 multiple occurrences, 238 occur only twice. Thus only 463 words (23.8 percent) occur three or more times. The figures are based on the tables in P. Bouet and others, Konokordanz zu den Satiren des Persius Flaccus (Hildesheim, 1978).

6. The solemn imperative form -nto is used by Horace in a similar parody, Satire 2.1.8-9.

7. A useful and easily accessible selection is listed in the preface to D. Bo's Lexicon, p. viii. For nonpoetic vocabulary in general a standard work is B. Axelson, Unpoetische Wörter (Lund: Gleerup, 1945), especially chap. 3, pp. 46-97. See also V. Gerard, "Le latin vulgaire et le langage familier dans les satires de Perse," Le Musée Belge 1 (1897):81-103.

8. Aulus Gellius, Noctes Atticae, 16.7

9. Persius uses an intensive form vegrandis ("ultralarge") at 1.97, whose only other occurrence in poetry is in Lucilius, fr. 705 W. Cicero uses the word once, De Lege Agraria 2.34.93: cf. Horace's vepallida ("ultrapale") at Satire 1.2.129, where the reading is doubtful. Harvey, A Commentary on Persius, and J. R. Jenkinson, Persius: the Satires (Warminster, England 1980), notes to 1.97, prefer "stunted" (that is, vegrandis = "undersized"), and are supported by the Oxford Latin Dictionary (s.v. vegrandis) and by Warmington, note to Lucilius, fr. 705 W. Another intensive compound is praegrandis, used by Persius at Satire 1.124.

10. Plautus, Mercator 416. See the Oxford Latin
Dictionary for primary meanings.
11. The idea of the purified ear of the good
philosophical disciple is repeated in the fifth satire,
lines 63 and 86. Compare Lucilius, fr. 690 W.
12. Pellis ("skin") is used at 4.14, and its
diminutive, pellicula at 5.116. It was used by Horace
(also with reference to sunbathing) in Satire 2.5.38.
Juvenal imitates Persius's word cuticula in Satire
11.203, again with reference to sunburn but without
pejorative connotations.
13. Aristophanes, Equites 726 and 1199.
14. Aqualiculus is technically the lower stomach
and is so used by Seneca, Epistle 90.22. According to
the seventh century writer, Isidore, the word properly
referred to a pig's belly (Origines 11.1).
15. Horace, Ars Poetica 47-48: "dixeris egregie
notum si callida verbum/reddiderit iunctura novum"
("you will have spoken with distinction if a cunning
juxtaposition makes a common word fresh").
16. Cicero, De Oratore 3.160.
17. Horace, Satire 1.4.96-100.
18. "Soft" poetry (tenerum) at 1.98; "soft"
mouths or ears at 1.35 and 107. The synonym mollis is
used of contemporary metrical usage at 1.63.
19. Seneca, Epistle 114.15.
20. S. Johnson, Life of Cowley, in
Lives of the English Poets, ed. A. Waugh (London:
Oxford University Press, 1964) 1:14.
21. The best-known use of examen is in Vergil's
picture of Jupiter holding the scales of Destiny in the
Aeneid, 12.725. Persius must have had the epic model
in mind as he used the word ironically in Satire 1.6.
22. Plato, Theaetetus 179d; Horace, Epistle
2.2.8.
23. Persius uses excutere eight times, making it
one of his commonest verbs. It is used metaphorically
of moral or literary criticism at 1.49 and 118 as well
as here.
24. This is the obvious interpretation. Casaubon
prefers to see the grandmothers as metaphors for pride
in one's ancestry (a notorious fault of Roman nobles
and attacked by Persius in the fourth satire). Rudd
sees a pun on the word avia (a kind of weed) and translates "those weedy old misconceptions." Both inter-

pretations are too forced to be likely.
   25. Juvenal, among others, imitated this phrase,
Satire 6.165. The Oxford Dictionary of Quotations
attributes the phrase to Juvenal. Horace had used it
of the peacock, in a nonmetaphorical sense, at Satire
2.2.26.
   26. G. E. Duckworth, "Five Centuries of Latin
Hexameter Poetry: Silver Age and Late Empire,"
T.A.P.A. 98 (1967):77-150 (pp. 109-15 for Persius, with
the table on p. 146).
   27. Abraham Cowley, "The Dangers of Procrastina-
tion," in Essays in Verse and Prose, ed. J. R. Lumby
and A. Tilley (Cambridge: Cambridge University Press,
1923), p. 105. Cowley goes on to quote, as an "odd
expression . . . full of Fancy," Satire 5.68-69. The
quotation from Cowley is the epigraph of the excellent
discussion of poetic obscurity by John Press, The
Chequer'd Shade (Oxford: Oxford University Press,
1958), who also quotes the passages by Goethe and
Ruskin (p. 106).
   28. Ezra Pound, "How to Read," in Literary
Essays of Ezra Pound, ed. T. S. Eliot (London: Faber,
1954), p. 25. Pound's terminology is made up of the
Greek roots -poeia ("making"); melo- ("music" or
"song"); phano- ("appearance" or "image"); logo-
("word").
   29. Ezra Pound, "Irony, Laforgue, and Some
Satire," in Literary Essays, p. 283.
   30. Dryden, Discourse p. 247. The whole passage
(pp. 247-53) still deserves careful attention.

Chapter Seven

   1. Quintilian, 10.1.94; Martial, 4.29.7.
   2. For Persius and the Christian Fathers see H.
Hagendahl, Latin Fathers and the Classics (Göteborg:
University of Göteborg, 1958), especially pp. 145, 284.
   3. Augustine, De Civitate Dei 2.6 (Persius,
Satire 3.66-72); Epistle 132 (Satire 5.22-24). A full
list of quotations is given by H. Hagendahl,
Augustine and the Latin Classics, 2 vols. (Göteborg:
Almquist & Wiksell, 1967); see especially 1.215-18 and
2.472-74.
   4. For Jerome's satire see D. Wiesen, St.
Jerome as a Satirist (Ithaca: Cornell University

Press, 1964). For his use of Persius, see Hagendahl, Latin Fathers, pp. 145, 284.

5. This is the famous Pithoeanus (named from its sixteenth-century owner Pierre Pithou), now in the library of the medical school at Montpellier. It is also the principal manuscript for the text of Juvenal. For a description see Clausen's edition of Persius (Oxford, 1956) and the edition of Bo (Turin, 1969).

6. O Curas hominum is no. 187 in the Hilka-Schumann edition, and is on folio 83R of the manuscript. Although the manuscript includes musical notations for this poem, it is not one of the poems included in Orff's Carmina Burana. The medieval quotations of Persius are conveniently listed by M. Manitius, "Beiträge zur Geschichte römischer Dichter im Mittelalter," Philologus 47 (1888):710-20. For Germany there is a full treatment by G. F. Hering, Persius: Geschichte seines Nachlebens und seiner Übersetzungen in der deutschen Literatur, Germanischer Studien, vol. 165 (Berlin, 1935).

7. Purgatorio, 22.100. See also E. Paratore, "Echi di Persio nella Divina Commedia," in Biografia e Poetica di Persio (Florence, 1968).

8. The bibliography of M. H. Morgan (Cambridge, 1909) is excellent for the printed texts, commentaries, and translations of Persius before 1900. Morgan is especially informative about the early texts and editions of Persius; for example, he describes sixty-one incunabula (that is, editions printed before 1501). For Persius in the Middle Ages and the Renaissance see D. M. Robathan and F. E. Cranz, A. Persius Flaccus, in Catalogus Translationum et Commentariorum: Mediaeval and Renaissance Latin Translations and Commentaries (Washington, D. C., 1976), 3:201-312.

9. J. C. Scaliger, Poetices Libri Septem (Lyons, 1561). The quotations here translated are taken from this edition, bk. 3, chap. 98 (p. 149) and bk. 6, chap. 6 (p. 323). The selection from Scaliger's Poetics by F. M. Padelford, Select Translations from Scaliger's Poetics (New Haven: Yale University Press, 1905- Yale Studies in English 26 [1898]), does not include these passages.

10. Dryden, A Discourse, pp. 250-52.

11. The edition of Régnier's Oeuvres Complètes by G. Raibaud (Paris, 1958) has a useful list of Régnier's

sources and allusions, pp. 281-89. It contains only
one imitation of Persius (Régnier, Satire 4.8 from
Persius, 5.62, wrongly given by Raibaud as 4.62). See
above, chap. 3, n. 3, for another allusion.

12. Quotations from Boileau are taken from the
two-volume text of J. Vercruysse and S. Menant (Paris:
Garnier-Flammarion, 1969). A useful general survey
with bibliography is J. E. White, Nicolas Boileau (New
York: Twayne, 1969). The article by R. E. Colton,
"Echoes of Persius in Boileau," Latomus 35 (1976):851-
56, is disappointing. Besides the passages in
Boileau's eighth and ninth satires discussed here
Colton also sees imitations of Persius in the third and
fifth satires.

13. Discourse, p. 252, 266-67 respectively.
Dryden's flattery of his patron, Lord Dorset, should be
disregarded.

14. Epistle to Dr. Arbuthnot, pp. 69-82. Pope
was less circumspect than Persius in attacking the
monarch, his wife, and his chief minister.

15. References are to G. Sherburn, The Correspon-
dence of Alexander Pope, 5 vols. (Oxford: Oxford University Press, 1956). Pope quotes Persius 5.41-44 in
the letter to Cromwell of 12 October 1710 (Sherburn,
1:99), and in the letter to Broome of 24 April 1724
(Sherburn, 2:231), from which the quotation is taken.
In 1728 he wrote thanking Thomas Sheridan for his
(prose) translation of Persius (Sherburn 2:523), and in
1734 he praised Persius's freedom of speech in a letter
to Arbuthnot (Sherburn 3:420). Pope's interest in
Persius was maintained over many years.

16. Dryden's note 4 to his translation of
Persius's sixth satire. This comes on pp. 598-99 of J.
Sargeaunt's edition of The Poems of John Dryden
(Oxford: Oxford University Press, 1910), and often
reprinted. Dryden's suggestion that Lucan helped
Persius in these passages is without merit.

17. Letter to Jefferson of 17 July 1771:
references are taken from A Virginia Gentleman's
Library, a pamphlet edited by A. P. Middleton and
published at Colonial Williamsburg, 1972 (see The
Papers of Thomas Jefferson, ed. Julian Boyd [Princeton:
Princeton University Press, 1950] 1.74-75, 76-81).
Jefferson replied on 3 August 1771: his catalog
included translations of Seneca (under "Religion") and

Lucan (in Rowe's works, listed under "Fine Arts").
Neither Horace nor Juvenal is mentioned. The latter,
along with Persius, would have been available in
Dryden's works, which were listed.

18. The English verse-translations, except for
that of Rudd, are discussed in an engaging article by
W. Frost, "English Persius: The Golden Age,"
Eighteenth-Century Studies 2 (1968):77-101.

Selected Bibliography

PRIMARY SOURCES

1. Texts

A. Persi Flacci Saturarum Liber. Edited by W. V.
Clausen. Oxford: Clarendon Press, 1956. Includes
preface in English with discussion of the manuscript
tradition.

A. Persi Flacci et D. Iuni Iuvenalis Saturae. Edited
by W. V. Clausen. Oxford: Clarendon Press, 1959.
The standard modern edition in the Oxford Classical
Text series, with Latin preface.

A. Persii Flacci Saturarum Liber; cum Scholiis Antiquis.
Edited by O. Jahn. 1843. Reprint. Hildesheim:
Olms, 1967. The only available collection of the
scholia: revised in the Teubner editions of F.
Buecheler (1893) and F. Leo (1910). See W. V.
Clausen's criticisms, p. xiv of his 1956 edition and
p. viii of his 1959 edition, for the unsatisfactory
nature of Jahn's collection.

2. Editions and Commentaries

Bo, D. A. Persii Flacci Saturarum Liber. Turin:
Paravia, 1969. Latin preface and commentary with a
good bibliography. The most useful modern edition.

Casaubon, I. A. Persii Flacci Satirarum Liber. 3d ed.
Revised and enlarged by Meric Casaubon. London:
Flesher, 1647. First published in Paris, 1605. The
edition of 1695 was edited and reissued by F. Dueb-
ner (Leipzig: Lehnhold, 1833) and later reprinted
(Osnabrück: Biblio Verlag, 1972). Casaubon's
introduction and Latin commentary are the foundation
upon which all subsequent commentaries rest. His
edition also contains an important comparison of
Persius and Horace.

Conington, J. The Satires of A. Persius Flaccus. 3d
ed. Edited by H. Nettleship, 1874. Reprint.
Hildesheim: Olms, 1967. Long the standard English
edition, relying heavily upon Casaubon. Includes a

123

pedestrian prose translation.
Harvey, R. A. <u>A Commentary on Persius</u>. <u>Mnemosyne</u>,
supp. 64. Leiden: Brill, 1981. Full and detailed
commentary (without text), which will become the
standard English commentary. Generally balanced in
its judgments, it discusses the difficult passages
clearly and helpfully. Shows more discrimination
than its fullest predecessors, Villeneuve and
Beikircher (satire 6 only). Good references for
sources and parallels. The general introduction is
too brief to be helpful.
Jenkinson, J. R. <u>Persius: the Satires</u>. Warminster,
England: Aris & Phillips, 1980. Text (including
the <u>Vita</u>) with a prose translation and notes on
disputed passages. There is a short general introduction and quite full appendixes on satires 1, 3-4,
and 6. The commentary is not generally as lucid as
that of Harvey. The translation of Rudd and the
commentary of Harvey are preferable. Both Harvey
and Jenkinson have bibliographies.
Neméthy, G. <u>A. Persii Flacci Satirae</u>. Budapest:
Hungarian Academy, 1923. An excellent Latin Commentary with index verborum: also separate notes on
twenty-six passages ("Symbolae Exegeticae ad Persii
Satiras").
Scivoletto, N. <u>Auli Persi Flacci Saturae</u>. 2d ed.
Florence: La Nuova Italia, 1961. A reliable text
and Italian commentary.
Seel, O. <u>Die Satiren des Persius</u>. 2d ed. Munich:
Heimeran, 1974. Text and German hexameter transla-
tion with sympathetic essay on Persius, notes, and
discussion of the manuscript tradition. Brief
bibliography.
Villeneuve, F. <u>Les Satires de Perse</u>. Paris:
Hachette, 1918. The fullest modern commentary.

3. Translations
Conington, J. (see under editions and commentaries).
Prose translation: literal and without any claims
to style.
Dryden, J. In <u>The Poems of John Dryden</u>. Edited by J.
Sargeaunt. Oxford: Oxford University Press, 1910.
Often reprinted. Heroic couplets, whose formality
is too confining for Persius's style. Although it
suffers in comparison to Dryden's translation of
Juvenal (whom he found far more congenial) this is

still the best verse translation and it set the standard for English translations for two centuries.

Jenkinson, J. R. (see under editions and commentaries). A more modern prose translation than that of Conington, but equally lacking in literary qualities.

Merwin, W. S. The Satires of Persius. Introduction and notes by W. S. Anderson. Bloomington: Indiana University Press, 1961. A lively modern blank-verse version, of great literary merit.

Rudd, N. The Satires of Horace and Persius. Harmondsworth: Penguin, 1973. A six-beat blank-verse version by one of the foremost modern scholars in Latin satire. Readable and accurate, with an excellent introduction. The best for readers being introduced to Persius.

4. Concordances

Bo, D. Auli Persii Flacci Lexicon. Hildesheim: Olms, 1967. Much more useful than the Index Verborum of L. Berkowitz and T. F. Brunner (Hildesheim: Olms, 1967). Lists words with references and Latin definitions, including variant manuscript readings. An indispensable aid to study of Persius.

Bouet, P., Callebat, L., Fleury, P., and Zuinghedau, M. Konkordanz zu den Satiren des Persius Flaccus. Hildesheim: Olms, 1978. Lists words alphabetically with context: contains frequency-counts under grammatical categories of words. Good bibliography. For the standard German bibliographies see p. 9.

SECONDARY SOURCES

1. Bibliographies

Anderson, W. S. "Recent Work on Roman Satire," Classical World (formerly Classical Weekly) 50 (1956):37-38; 57 (1964):344-46; 63 (1970):191-99; 5 (1982):285-88. The pages cited are concerned only with Persius: Anderson's articles are useful for work on the whole field of Roman Satire in the last forty years.

D'Agostino, V. Gli Studi su Persio dal 1932 al 1946. Rassegna Bibliografica. Turin: Società editrice internazionale, 1947.

_____. "Nuova Bibliografia su Persio (1946-57)." R.S.C. 6 (1958):63-72.

_____. "Gli Studi su Persio dal 1957 at 1962. Nota

Bibliografica," R.S.C. II (1963):54-64.
Morgan, M. H. A Bibliography of Persius. Cambridge,
Mass.: Library of Harvard University, 1909. Lists
1,029 editions, translations, and secondary works,
two thirds of them in the author's own collection.
Especially useful for the early editions of Persius,
for which Morgan supplies quite detailed descriptions and eight facsimiles. The basic reference
work for Persius's standing in the Renaissance.
Robathan, D. M., and Cranz F. E. Catalogus Translationum et Commentariorum: Mediaeval and Renaissance
Latin Translations and Commentaries. 3:201-312.
A. Persius Flaccus. Washington, D.C.: Catholic
University Press, 1976. Invaluable reference work
for the fortunes of Persius in the period from late
antiquity through the Renaissance. Includes bibli-
ographical references and a catalogue raisonné of
all commentaries on Persius down to that of Farnaby
(1612).
Scivoletto, N. "Gli Studi su Persio negli ultimi
vent'anni," Cultura e Scuola 7 (1963):58-65. A
critical survey of selected articles.

2. Books
a. Roman Satire in General
Coffey, M. Roman Satire. London: Methuen, and New
York: Barnes and Noble, 1976. By far the most
reliable book in the field, although the author is
often too restrained. Each area (author or genre)
is dealt with separately, with summary of works,
discussion of style and other literary questions,
survey of manuscript tradition and influence. There
are full notes with references to the relevant
scholarship. Especially useful is the second
chapter on the origins of Roman satire. The sixth
chapter, on Persius, is rather unsympathetic to the
poet, but judicious in assessing the secondary
literature.
Highet, G. The Anatomy of Satire. Princeton:
Princeton University Press, 1962. A selective
survey over the whole range of European satire:
somewhat superficial, but important as a classical
scholar's view of the principles of the genre of
satire. Chapter 2, on diatribe, is especially
useful.
Krenkel, W., ed. Römische Satire. Wissenschaftliche

Zeitschrift der Universitat Rostock, Gesellschaft- und Sprachwissenschaftliche Reihe 15, pts. 4-5, pp. 407-584. Rostock, 1966. Twenty essays on Roman satire, each with a summary in English. W. S. Anderson's (see below) and Krenkel's conributions on Persius (respectively pp. 409-16 and 471-77) are good, although they take different views of Per- sius's attitude to Roman society. Useful also is U. W. Scholz on the fourth satire, pp. 525-31.

Knoche, U. Die römische Satire. 4th ed. Göttingen, 1982. Translated by E. S. Ramage. Roman Satire. Bloomington: Indiana University Press, 1975. Still the standard survey of the subject, scholarly and balanced. Both the German edition (1982) and the American translation contain bibliographies. Chap- ter 10 is on Persius.

Korzeniewski, D., ed. Die römische Satire. Wege der Forschung, vol. 238. Darmstadt: Wissenschaftliche Buchgesellschaft, 1970. A collection of important articles on Roman satire in (or translated into) German, including those of Korzeniewski (on Per- sius's first satire) and Henss listed below.

Puelma Piwonka, M. Lucilius und Kallimachos. Frankfurt: Klostermann, 1949. An excellent survey of the Hellenistic satirical tradition and its rela- tionship to Roman satire.

Rudd, N. The Satires of Horace. Cambridge: Cambridge University Press, 1966. The best book on Horace's satires, containing much that is applicable to satire in general. An appendix has an important essay on Dryden's Discourse which does much to set the record straight after centuries of domination by the views of Dryden.

Schanz, M., and Hosius, C. Geschichte der römischen Literatur. Pt. 2. 4th ed. Munich: Beck, 1967. Müller's Handbuch der Altertumswissenschaft, 8:2. "Schanz-Hosius" is the basic handbook for Latin literary history: pp. 477-84 (sections 382-84) deal with Persius. It provides the basic source material and bibliographies through 1935, the original date for the fourth edition. Its judgments on Persius are harsh and quite wide of the mark, but as a reference book it is still the most useful. Else- where are sections devoted to certain figures in Persius's life, for example, Remmius Palaemon (sec- tion 475); Verginius Flavus (480);

Servilius Nonianus (440); Cornutus (451); Caesius
Bassus (385).
Sullivan, J. P. ed. Satire: Critical Essays on Roman
Literature. Bloomington: Indiana University Press,
1968. Four essays on Horace, Persius, Petronius,
and Juvenal. Stimulating and at times controver-
sial: see below for Nisbet's essay on Persius.

b. Historical Background
Levi, M. A. Nerone e I Suoi Tempi. Milan: Instituto
Editoriale Cisalpino, 1949. Still the best account
of Nero's reign, with an interesting examination of
the reasons for Nero's failure. Concentrates upon the
first part of the reign (that is, before the death
of Persius), and integrates the cultural and literary aspects with the political and economic.
Scullard, H. H. From the Gracchi to Nero. 3d ed.
London: Methuen, 1970. A reliable history of the
period from 133 B.C. to 68 A.D. (the end of the
reign of Nero).
Warmington, B. H. Nero: Reality and Legend. London:
Chatto and Windus, 1969. A good assessment of the
age of Nero with a commonsense approach to the
problem of separating legend from fact.

c. On Persius
Beikircher, H. Kommentar zur VI. Satire des A. Persius
Flaccus. Wiener Studien, supp. 1. Vienna, 1969. A
detailed commentary on the sixth satire.
Bramble, J. C. Persius and the Programmatic Satire.
Cambridge: Cambridge University Press. 1974. A
close analysis of the first satire and its place in
the satiric tradition. It is written in a very
difficult style and unduly emphasizes sexual
imagery. These defects lessen the value of the
author's deep knowledge of the scholarship on the
satiric tradition.
Ciresola, T. La Formazione del Linguaggio Poetico di
Persio. Rovereto: Longo, 1953. A rather summary
treatment of aspects of Persius's style and vocabulary, with useful, if selective, lists.
Dessen, Cynthia S. Iunctura Callidus Acri. Illinois
Studies in Language and Literature, no. 59. Urbana:
University of Illinois Press, 1968. The only readable book on Persius in English, but generally disappointing because of the overemphasis on dominant

metaphors. More useful to those who prefer the literary-critical approach, it contains some good material on the relationship of satire 4 to the Sokratikoi Logoi. Those who can penetrate Bramble's prose will learn more from his book.

Hering, G. F. Persius: Geschichte seines Nachlebens und seiner Übersetzungen in der deutschen Literatur. Germanische Studien, vol. 165. Berlin: Ebering, 1935. The only full-length study of Persius's influence. Despite its title it contains good remarks on non-German authors, including Casaubon and Dryden.

Paratore, E. Biografia e Poetica di Persio. Florence: Le Monnier, 1968. Often wordy and polemical, but containing reprints of some significant articles by Paratore, including one on Persius and Lucan and two on Dante and Persius.

Scritti per il xix Centenario della Nascita di Persio. Biblioteca della Rassegna Volterrana, no. 3. Volterra, Italy: Accademia dei Sepolti, 1936. A collection of essays by Italian scholars on different aspects of Persius and his work. See below for the articles by Festa and Terzaghi.

Villeneuve, F. Essai sur Perse. Paris: Hachette, 1918. An exhaustive study of every aspect of Persius's work.

3. Articles

Anderson, W. S. "Part versus Whole in Persius' Fifth Satire." Philological Quarterly 39 (1960):66-81. Studies the structure of the fifth satire, which is a unity despite Persius's failure to link the subordinate parts.

_____. "Persius and the Rejection of Society." In Rostock, pp. 409-16. Shows how Persius as a Stoic poet rejects society because he does not accept its values. A useful article for Persius's persona and poetic techniques. Anderson's articles have been reprinted in Essays on Roman Satire (Princeton: Princeton University Press, 1982).

D'Agostino, V. "I Diminutivi in Persio," Atti di Reale Accademia de Scienze Torino (Classe morali storiche et filosofiche) 63 (1927-28):5-23. Lists all of Persius's diminutives with notes on each. A valuable article for Persius's style.

Duckworth, G. E. "Five Centuries of Latin Hexameter

Poetry: Silver Age and Late Empire," T.A.P.A. 98
(1967):77-150. Pages 109-15 for Persius, with
tables on p. 146. Gives statistical comparisons of
the metrical practices of the satirists.

Faranda, G. "Caratteristiche dello stile e del
linguaggio poetico di Persio." Rendiconti dell'
Istituto Lombardo (Cl. lett. e sc. mor. e stor.) 88
(1955):512-38. A good general article on Persius's
style.

Festa, N. "Persio e Cleante." In Volterra Scritti,
pp. 15-30. Very helpful for Persius's Stoic attitudes, especially as seen in the fifth satire.

Frost, W. "English Persius: The Golden Age."
Eighteenth Century Studies 2 (1968):77-101. Discusses twelve English translations of Persius from
Holyday (1616) to Merwin (1961). Instructive for
problems of interpreting Persius's style in English,
and useful for the history of taste in attitudes
toward Latin satire.

Gerard, V. "Le latin vulgaire et le langage familier
dans les satires de Perse." Le Musée Belge 1
(1897):81-103. The only adequate treatment of Persius's use of Vulgar Latin: examines vocabulary,
syntax, usage, and metaphors derived from common
speech and actions.

Henss, D. "Die Imitationstechnik des Persius."
Philologus 99 (1955):277-94. Reprinted in Korzeniewski, Die römische Satire, pp. 365-83. Important for Persius's use of Horace. More accessible
and more critical than Casaubon's basic Persiana
Horatii Imitatio, which was included in his edition
of Persius.

Housman, A. E. "Notes on Persius." C. Q. 7 (1913):12-
32. Notes on sixteen passages, written in Housman's
usual acerbic style. Very helpful for interpretation of difficult places in Persius.

Kenney, E. J. "The First Satire of Juvenal."
Proceedings of the Cambridge Philological Society, 8
(1962):29-40. The basic article on the program
satires of Horace, Persius, and Juvenal. Excellent
for the influence of Persius's first satire on
Juvenal's first satire.

Korzeniewski, D. "Die erste Satire des Persius." In
Die römische Satire, pp. 384-438. Analysis of the
structure and purpose of the first satire: more
lucid than Bramble's book.

Kroll, W. "Persius." In R-E., supp. 7, cols. 972-79.
Basic article for all aspects of Persius's work and
influence.
Manitius, M. "Beiträge zur Geschichte römischer
Dichter im Mittelalter." Philologus 47 (1888):710-
20. The basic listing of citations from Persius in
medieval authors.
_____. "Philologisches aus alten Bibliothekskatalogen
(bis 1300)." Rheinisches Museum 47, supp. (1892).
Pages 52-54 deal with Persius, listing the manu-
scripts to be found in medieval monastic libraries.
Useful for the history of Persius during the Middle
Ages.
Martin, J. M. K. "Persius--Poet of the Stoics."
Greece and Rome 8 (1939):172-82. A sensitive appre-
ciation of Persius and a good general introduction.
Nisbet, R. G. M. "Persius." In Critical Essays, ed.
Sullivan, pp. 39-71 (see above). The best general
essay on Persius, sympathetic and perceptive.
Reckford, K. J. "Studies in Persius." Hermes 90
(1962):476-504. Discusses aspects of Persius's use
of imagery; his Stoicism; the choliambics. Written
with discernment, this article is very informative
about Persius's poetic techniques in general, beyond
the few passages examined in detail.
Scivoletto, N. "La'Poetica'di Persio." In
Argentea Aetas: In Memoriam E. V. Marmorale.
Genoa: Universita di Genova Pubblicazioni Ist. di
Fil. Class. 37 (1973):83-106. A good essay on
Persius's poetic style, especially helpful on the
meaning of iunctura callidus acri (Satire 5.14).
Seel, O. "Zum Persius-Titel des Codex Pithoeanus."
Hermes 88 (1960):82-98. Argues for an "open" manuscript tradition for Persius, that is, without the
usual stemmata. An important article for understanding the history of the manuscripts of Persius.
Sullivan, J. P. "In Defence of Persius." Ramus 1
(1972):48-62. A stimulating introduction to Persius
with a valuable review of attitudes toward Persius,
including those of Casaubon, Dryden, and Donne, and
with a fair assessment of some modern scholarship.
Terzaghi, N. "La Terza Satira di Persio." In
Volterra Scritti, pp. 85-97. The most illuminating
article on the third satire: disposes of Hendrick-
son's reordering of the lines (in Classical Philolo-
gy 23 [1928]:97-112) and considers Persius's

sources, especially Lucilius and Horace.

Waszink, J. H. "Das Einleitungsgedicht des Persius." Wiener Studien 76 (1963):79-91. By far the best article on the choliambics: reviews the scholarship and argues cogently for approaching the choliambics as a poetic unity.

Index

133